JACQUES RANCIÈRE: EDUCATION, TRUTH, EMANCIPATION

JACQUES RANCIÈRE: EDUCATION, TRUTH, EMANCIPATION

CHARLES BINGHAM AND GERT J.J. BIESTA,
WITH JACQUES RANCIÈRE

continuum

Continuum International Publishing Group

The Tower Building   80 Maiden Lane
11 York Road   Suite 704
London SE1 7NX   New York, NY 10038

www.continuumbooks.com

© Charles Bingham and Gert Biesta, 2010

British Library Cataloguing-in-Publication Data
A catalogue record for this book is available from the British Library.

ISBN: HB: 978-1-4411-9095-6
         PB: 978-1-4411-3216-1

Library of Congress Cataloging-in-Publication Data
Bingham, Charles W. (Charles Wayne)
Jacques Rancière : education, truth, emancipation / Charles Bingham
and Gert J.J. Biesta, with Jacques Rancière.
p. cm.
Includes bibliographical references (p.).
ISBN 978-1-4411-9095-6 – ISBN 978-1-4411-3216-1
1. Rancière, Jacques–Philosophy. 2. Education–Philosophy.
I. Biesta, Gert. II. Rancière, Jacques. III. Title.
LB880.R352B56 2010
370.1–dc22

2010004173

Typeset by Newgen Imaging Systems Pvt Ltd, Chennai, India
Printed and bound in Great Britain by CPI Antony Rowe,
Chippenham, Wiltshire

CONTENTS

CHAPTER 1

ON IGNORANT SCHOOLMASTERS[1]

by Jacques Rancière

We are gathered here to speak on the qualities of schoolmasters. I have written a work called *The Ignorant Schoolmaster* (Rancière 1991a). It is thus logically up to me to defend a most unreasonable position: That the most important quality of a schoolmaster is the virtue of ignorance. My book recounts the history of a teacher, Joseph Jacotot, who caused quite a scandal in Holland and France of the 1830s. He did so by proclaiming that uneducated people could learn on their own, without a teacher explaining things to them, and that teachers, for their part, could teach what they themselves were ignorant of. In addition to the risk of dealing in simplistic paradoxes, there is, then, the added risk of revelling in the old-fashioned ideas and exaggerations of pedagogical history. I would like to show, though, that it is not a matter of taking pleasure in paradox, but of fundamental inquiry into the meanings of knowledge, teaching and learning; not an amusing journey into the history of pedagogy, but a matter of timely philosophical reflection on the way in which pedagogical logic and social logic bear on each other.

So, let me get to the heart of the question. What is this quality, this virtue, of ignorance? What is an ignorant schoolmaster? To respond well to this question, it is necessary to distinguish between a few different levels. At the most immediate empirical level, an ignorant schoolmaster is a teacher who teaches that which is unknown to him or her. It is thus that Joseph Jacotot unexpectedly found himself, in the 1820s, teaching Flemish students whose language he did not know and who did not know his, by using a fortuitous text, a bilingual edition of *Télémaque* being published in Brussels. He put it in his students' hands and told them, through an interpreter, to read

1

half of the book with the aid of the translation, to constantly repeat what they had learned, to read the other half quickly, and to write in French what they thought of it. He was said to be astonished at the way these students, to whom he had not transmitted any knowledge, had, following his command, learned enough French to express themselves very well, how he had thus educated them without teaching them anything. From this, he concluded that the act of the teacher who obliges another intelligence to exercise itself was independent of the possession of knowledge, that it was indeed possible that one who is ignorant might permit another who is ignorant to know something unknown to both, possible that a common, illiterate person might, for example, permit another illiterate person to learn to read.

And there is a second level to the question, a second sense of the expression 'ignorant schoolmaster': An ignorant schoolmaster is not an ignorant person who is thrilled by playing teacher. It is a teacher who teaches – that is to say who is for another a means of knowledge – without transmitting any knowledge. It is thus a teacher who enacts a dissociation between the mastery of the schoolmaster and his or her knowledge, who shows us that the so-called 'transmission of knowledge' consists in fact of two intertwined relations that are important to dissociate: a relation of will to will and a relation of intelligence to intelligence. But, one must not be wrong about the meaning of this dissociation. There is the usual way of understanding it: the desire to undermine the relation of educational authority in order that one intelligence might enlighten another more effectively. Such is the principle of numerous anti-authoritarian pedagogies whose model is the maieutic of the Socratic pedagogue, of the pedagogue who feigns ignorance in order to provoke knowledge. But, the ignorant schoolmaster conducts this dissociation in a different manner. He or she indeed knows the double gambit of the maieutic. Under the guise of creating a capacity, the maieutic aims, in fact, to demonstrate an incapacity. Socrates not only shows the incapacity of false savants, but also the incapacity of whoever is not lead by the teacher down the right path, through the proper relation of intelligence to intelligence. The 'liberalist' maieutic is just a sophisticated variation of ordinary pedagogical practice, which entrusts to the teacher's intelligence the ability to bridge the gap separating the ignorant person from knowledge. Jacotot inverts the meaning of this dissociation: The ignorant schoolmaster exercises no relation of intelligence to intelligence. He or she is only an authority, only a will that sets the ignorant

2

person down a path, that is to say to instigate a capacity already possessed, a capacity that every person has demonstrated by succeeding, without a teacher, at the most difficult of apprenticeships: The apprenticeship of that foreign language that is, for every child arriving in the world, called his or her mother tongue.

Such is indeed the lesson of a chance experience that made the learned teacher Jacotot into an ignorant schoolmaster. This lesson bears on the very logic of pedagogical reasoning, on its aims and its means. The usual aim of pedagogical logic is to teach the student that which he or she doesn't know, to close the gap between the ignorant one and knowledge. Its usual means is explanation. To explain is to arrange the elements of knowledge to be transmitted in accordance with the supposed limited capacities of those under instruction. But, such a simple idea of being in accordance shows itself to be characterized by infinite regress. An explanation is generally accompanied by an explanation of that explanation. Books are necessary to explain to students the knowledge to be learned. But, such explanation is apparently insufficient: Teachers are still needed to explain, to those who are ignorant, the books that explain this knowledge. Explanations are needed so that the one who is ignorant might understand the explanation that enables his or her understanding. The regress would be in principle infinite if the teacher's authority did not in fact stop it by acting as sole arbiter of the endpoint where explanations are no longer needed. Jacotot believed that he could sum up the logic of this apparent paradox. If explanation is in principle infinite, it is because its primary function is to infinitize the very distance it proposes to reduce.

The practice of explanation is something completely different from a practical means of reaching some end. It is an end in itself, the infinite verification of a fundamental axiom: the axiom of inequality. To explain something to one who is ignorant is, first and foremost, to explain that which would not be understood if it were not explained. It is to demonstrate an incapacity. Explanation offers itself as a means to reduce the situation of inequality where those who know nothing are in relation with those who know. But, this reduction is, rather, a confirmation. To explain assumes that the material to be learned has a specific sort of opacity, an opacity that resists the types of interpretation and imitation used by a child, a child who can already translate the signs received from the world and from the speaking beings around him or her.

Such is the particular inequality that normal pedagogical logic orchestrates. This orchestration has three particular traits. First, it supposes a radical distinction between two types of intelligences: On one hand, the empirical intelligence of speaking beings who speak and interpret one another; on the other, the systematic intelligence of those who understand things according to their particular articulations: For children and common minds there are stories, for rational beings there are reasons. Instruction thus appears as a radical point of departure, or a new birth, as soon as it not a matter of telling and interpreting, but of explaining and understanding. Instruction's first accomplishment is to split the intellect in two, to consign to the everyday life of students the procedures by which their minds have heretofore learned everything they know.

Then, its second feature: pedagogical logic appears as the act that lifts a veil off the obscurity of things. Its topography is that of top to bottom, of surface to depth. The explicator is the one who carries obscure depth to the clear surface, and who, conversely, brings the false appearance of the surface back to the secret depths of reason. This verticality distinguishes between the depths of reason's learned order, and the horizontal ways of the self-taught who move from proximity to proximity, comparing what they don't know to what they do know. Thirdly, this topography itself implies a certain temporality. Lifting the veil from things, bringing back the surface to its depth and bringing all depth to the surface, this not only requires time. It supposes a certain temporal order. The veil is lifted progressively, according to the ability attributed to the infantile mind, or to the one who knows nothing at this or that stage. In other words, progress always goes hand in hand with a certain regress. A reduction in distance never ceases to reinstate, and to verify, the axiom of inequality.

Ordinary pedagogical logic is supported by two fundamental axioms: First, one must start from inequality in order to reduce it; second, the way to reduce inequality is to conform to it by making of it an object of knowledge. The success of knowledge that reduces inequality works through a knowledge of inequality. This is the 'knowledge' that the ignorant schoolmaster refuses. It is the third sense of his or her ignorance. It is ignorance of this 'knowledge of inequality' that is supposed to prepare the way to 'reduce' inequality. About inequality, there is nothing to know. Inequality is no more a given to be transformed by knowledge than equality is an end to be transmitted through knowledge. Equality and inequality are not two states. They are two 'opinions', that is to say two

4

distinct axioms, by which educational training can operate, two axioms that have nothing in common. All that one can do is verify the axiom one is given. The schoolmaster's explanatory logic presents inequality axiomatically. Following this logic, there is inequality among minds but one can make use of this very inequality, putting it at the service of a future equality. The teacher is the non-equal who works to abolish his or her own privilege. The art of the schoolmaster, who methodically lifts the veil from that which the student could not understand alone, is the art that promises the student will one day be the equal of the schoolmaster. For Jacotot, this equality-to-come simply comprises the unequal equality which will, in turn, drive a system that produces and reproduces inequality. The overall logic of this process that presumes inequality, this logic merits for Jacotot the name of stultification.

The ignorant schoolmaster's logic poses equality as an axiom to be verified. It relates the state of inequality in the teacher-student relation not to the promise of an equality-to-come that will never come, but to the reality of a basic equality. In order for the ignorant one to do the exercises commanded by the master, the ignorant one must already understand what the master says. There is an equality of speaking beings that comes before the relation of inequality, one that sets the stage for inequality's very existence. This is what Jacotot calls the equality of intelligences. This does not mean that all the actions of all intelligences are the same. It means that there is only one intelligence at work in all intellectual training. The ignorant schoolmaster – that is to say one who is ignorant of inequality – addresses him or herself to the ignorant person not from the point of view of the person's ignorance but of the person's knowledge; the one who is supposedly ignorant in fact already understands innumerable things. He or she has learned them by listening and repeating, by observing and comparing, by guessing and verifying. This is how one's mother tongue is learned. It is how he or she can learn written language, for example, through comparing a prayer known by heart to the unfamiliar patterns that form, on paper, the written text of the same poem. One must have the student relate what he or she does not know to what is known, to observe and compare, to recount what has been seen and to verify what has been said. If there is a refusal to do this, it is because the student does not think it possible or necessary to know any more.

The obstacle stopping the abilities of the ignorant one is not his or her ignorance, but the consent to inequality. The ignorant one holds the opinion that intelligences are not equal.

But, this opinion is precisely not a matter of individual failure. It is a systemic axiom, an axiom by which the social system generally operates: the axiom of inequality. Those who do not want to develop their intellectual powers further are satisfied with not 'being able' to do so, satisfied with the assurance that others are even less able. The axiom of inequality is an axiom that underwrites inequalities operating on a societal scale. It is not the teacher's knowledge that can suspend the operation of this machine, but the teacher's will. The emancipatory teacher's call forbids the supposed ignorant one the satisfaction of what is known, the satisfaction of admitting that one is incapable of knowing more. Such a teacher forces the student to prove his or her capacity, to continue the intellectual journey the same way it began. This logic, operating under the presupposition of equality and requiring its verification, this logic deserves the name 'intellectual emancipation'.

The distinction between 'stultification' and 'emancipation' is not a distinction between methods of instruction. It is not a distinction between traditional or authoritarian methods, on the one hand, and new or active methods, on the other: stultification can and does happen in all kinds of active and modern ways. The distinction is properly one of philosophy. It concerns an idea of intelligence that guides the very conception of intellectual training. The axiom of equality of intelligences does not affirm any particular virtue for those who do not know, no science of the humble or intelligence of the masses. It simply affirms that there is only one sort of intelligence at work in all intellectual training. It is always a matter of relating what one ignores to what one knows; a matter of observing and comparing, of speaking and verifying. The student is always a seeker. And, the teacher is first of all a person who speaks to another, who tells stories and returns the authority of knowledge to the poetic condition of all spoken interaction. The philosophical distinction thus understood is, at the same time, a political distinction. It is not political because it would denounce high knowledge in the name of a common intelligence. It is at one level much more radical, because it concerns the very conception of the relation between equality and inequality.

It is indeed the very logic of the usual relation between these terms that Jacotot throws into question by denouncing the paradigm of explanation, showing that explanatory logic is a social logic; it is a way in which the social order is presented and reproduced. If this history of the 1830s concerns us directly, it is because it provides an exemplary response to the establishment of a new political system: a system where inequality is no longer supposed to rest on a realty that is sovereign or divine; a system, in short, of immanence, of the equalization of inequality. The years of the jacotist polemic indeed correspond to the moment when a reconstituted social order is being put into place after the upheaval of the French Revolution. It is a moment when one wants to achieve revolution, in all senses of the word 'achieve', to pass from the age of critique with its destruction of monarchical and divine transcendencies to the 'organic' age of a society based on its own, immanent reason. That is to say a society putting into harmony its productive forces, its institutions, and its beliefs, making them act according to a singular regime of rationality. Such is the grand project that cuts across the nineteenth century – understood not simply as a chronological break but as an historical project. Passing from the age of critique and revolution to an organic age is primarily about regulating the relation between equality and inequality. One must, said Aristotle, 'reveal democracy to democrats and oligarchy to oligarchs'.

The project of an organic modern society is the project of an unequal order that makes equality visible, which includes such visibility in the governing of relations between economic powers, institutions, and beliefs. It is the project of those 'mediations' that institute, between the top and bottom, two essential things: a minimum social fabric of common beliefs and the possibility for a limited movement among the levels of wealth and power. A plan for the 'people's education' is inscribed at the heart of this project, a plan that proceeds not only by the state organization of public instruction, but also by multiple philanthropic, commercial or community initiatives devoted to a twofold task: on one hand developing 'practical abilities', that is to say forms of rationalized, useful knowledges that permit people to leave their present circumstances, and to improve their conditions without actually leaving those conditions behind or denouncing them; on the other, enriching everyday life by allowing participation, in measured ways, in the pleasures of art while developing a sense of community: the 'aesthetic' education of the people modelled after the foundation of choral societies.

The vision of community that animates these various private and public initiatives is clear: A triple effect is obtained. First, to pull people away from retrograde practices and beliefs that keep them from participating in the increase of wealth and development, and that create resentment towards the ruling elites. Second, to establish, between elites and the people, a minimal common set of beliefs and pleasures that precludes a society fractured into two separate, and potentially hostile, worlds. Third, to assure a minimum of social mobility which gives to all the feeling of improvement, which allows the people's most gifted offspring to climb the social ladder and to participate in the ruling elite's renewal. Thus conceived, people's education is not simply an instrument, a practical means of working to reinforce the social order. It is actually an 'explanation' of society; it is a working allegory of the way that inequality is reproduced by 'making visible' equality.

This 'making visible' is not a simple illusion, it participates in a positivity I call the 'distribution of the sensible': an overall relation between ways of being, ways of doing and ways of saying. It is not the mask beneath which social inequality hides. It is the double-edged visibility of this inequality: inequality applied in the service of its own suppression, proving through its actions the incessant and unending nature of such suppression. Inequality does not hide beneath equality. Inequality has a way of asserting itself through equality. This equality of equality and inequality has a name. It is called progress. Organic, modern society, which sets itself the task of 'achieving' the revolution, sets the hierarchical order of ancient societies against the 'progressive' order, an order identical to mobility itself, to the movement of expansion, of transmission and application of knowledges. The school is not only the means towards this new progressive order. It is its very model: the model of an inequality which identifies itself with the visible difference between those who know and those who do not know and which devotes itself, visibly, to the task of teaching those who are ignorant that which they do not know, and thus reducing such inequality. But reducing by stages, according to the best methods known only to those who are unequal: methods that offer to a given population, at the opportune moment, the knowledge it is capable of acquiring for good use. Scholarly progression is the art of limiting the transmission of knowledge, of organizing delay, of deferring equality. The pedagogical paradigm of the master explicator, adapted to the level and needs of students, provides a model of the scholarly institution's social function, which itself translates to a general model of a society ordered by progress.

The ignorant schoolmaster is the teacher who escapes from this game, by separating the sheer act of intellectual emancipation from

ON IGNORANT SCHOOLMASTERS

the societal machine, and from progressive institutions. Distinguishing the act of intellectual emancipation from the institution of the people's instruction is to affirm that there are no stages to equality; that equality is a complete act or is not at all. There is a heavy price to pay for this escape. If explanation is a social method, the method by which inequality gets represented and reproduced, and if the institution is the place where this representation operates, it follows that intellectual emancipation is necessarily distinct from social and institutional logic. That is to say that there is no social emancipation, and no emancipatory school. Jacotot strictly distinguishes the method of emancipation, which is the method of individuals, from the social method of explanation. Society is a mechanism ruled by the momentum of unequal bodies, by the game of compensated inequalities. Equality can only be introduced therein at the price of inequality, by transforming equality into its opposite. Only individuals can be emancipated. And all emancipation can promise is to teach people to be equal in a society ruled by inequality and by the institutions that 'explain' such inequality.

This extreme paradox deserves to be taken seriously. It reminds us of two essential matters. First, that equality, in general, is not an end to be attained. It is a point of departure, a presupposition to be verified by sequences of specific acts. Secondly, equality sets the condition for inequality itself. To obey an order, one must understand that order, and one must understand that one must obey it. Thus, a minimum of equality is necessary without which inequality would not make sense. From these two axioms, Jacotot drew a radical dissociation: Emancipation can never be a social logic. I tried to show in *Disagreement* that this could be articulated otherwise, that the egalitarian condition of inequality could lend itself to sequences of acts, to forms of verification that were properly political (1999). But, that demonstration is not part of the theme that brings us here today. I will thus take up another aspect of the problem: How, today, to think about this relation between pedagogical logic and social logic that Jacotot put at the heart of his argument? At first glance, this relation presents itself today in the form of a strange dialectic. On one hand, the school sees itself incessantly accused of failing its task of reducing social inequality. But on the other, the school, constantly called inadequate to its social function, appears more and more as a suitable model for egalitarian functioning, that is to say for the unequal equality proper to our societies.

9

I will begin, in order to illustrate this dialectic, with the scholarly debate on equality and inequality as it has developed in France since the 1960s, since the terms of the debate appear to me to summarize, fairly well, a problem that one finds in the same form more or less everywhere. The debate was launched by Bourdieu's thesis that can be summed up as follows. The school is failing at its assigned mission of reducing inequalities, and this is because it ignores the functioning of inequality. It pretends to reduce inequality by distributing knowledge equally, and to all. But, it is precisely this appearance of equality that is the driving force behind educational inequality. It remains up to the students and their 'individual talents' to make a difference. But, these very talents are nothing but the cultural privileges of the children of well-to-do families. The children of the privileged classes do not want to know this, the children of the dominated classes cannot know this and the latter give up due to an acute awareness of their lack of talents. The school fails to enact equality because its egalitarian appearance hides the fact that inherited cultural capital has in fact been given the new face of individual difference.

But the school, according to this logic, functions unfairly because it does not know how inequality itself functions, because it does not wish to know. But this 'refusal to know' can be interpreted in two opposite ways. It can be understood as ignorance of the conditions of transforming inequality into equality. It is thus said that the teacher misunderstands the conditions of pedagogical practice because he or she lacks knowledge, the knowledge of inequality, knowledge that can be learned from the sociologist. The conclusion drawn is that educational inequality is remediable through a supplemental knowledge explaining the rules of the game, and rationalizing educational training. This was the conclusion of Bourdieu and Passeron in their first book, *The Inheritors*.

But, the refusal to know can also be understood as a successful interiorization of the logic of the system. It can thus also be said that the teacher is an agent in the process of the reproduction of cultural capital which, through a necessity inherent to the very functioning of the social machine, infinitely reproduces its conditions of possibility. Every program of reform thus appears immediately futile. It is in this vein that Bourdieu and Passeron conclude their next book, *Reproduction*. There is thus a duplicity in their argument. It concludes on one hand that there can be a reduction of inequality, and on the other that reproduction of inequality is perpetual. But this duplicity is none other than the duplicity of 'progressivism' itself, just as it was analysed by Jacotot. It is the logic of inequality that is reproduced by the very act of its own reduction. The sociologist introduces one more turn in the spiral by including one more ignorance, a supplementary incapacity: the ignorance of those who are supposed to do away with ignorance.

Government reformers are not fond of seeing this duplicity proper to all progressive pedagogy. From Bourdieu's sociology, socialist reformers thus would draw up a plan aiming to reduce educational inequalities by lessening education's focus on high culture, by making it less cerebral and more life-embracing, more adapted to the ways of being of children from unfavourable backgrounds, that is to say, for the most part, children of immigrants. This 'dumbed down' sociology only affirmed, unfortunately, all the more, the suppositions central to progressivism, suppositions ordering those who know to put themselves 'within reach' of those who are unequal, to limit the knowledge transmitted to that which the poor can understand and that which they need. It reproduces an approach that confirms present inequality in the name of an equality to come. This is why there had to be a backlash. In France, republican ideology was quick to denounce these methods adapted to the poor, which could never be but the methods of the poor, right away driving the 'dominated' back into the situation they were supposed to be helped out of. Instead, the power of equality resided, for republican ideology, in the universality of knowledge equally distributed to all, without consideration of social origin, in a school well-removed from society.

But, the distribution of knowledge does not, in itself, include any egalitarian consequences for the social order. Equality as well as inequality is never anything but the result of themselves. Traditional pedagogies of the neutral transmission of knowledge, as well as modernist pedagogies of knowledge adapted to societal conditions, cling to the same side of the alternative proposed by Jacotot. Both take equality as an end; that is to say, they take inequality as the point of departure and work under its presupposition. They diverge only on the sort of 'knowledge of inequality' they presuppose. Both of them are ensconced in the circle of a society pedagogicized. Both attribute to the school the fantasmatic power of realizing social equality or, at least, of reducing 'social fragmentation', even if it means taking turns denouncing the failure of the other to realize this program. Sociology calls this failure the 'crisis of the school' and it calls for school reform. Republicanism happily accuses reform itself of being the principal cause of the crisis. But, reform and crisis can lead to the same jacotist notion: Both are an explanation of school, a never-ending explanation of the reasons why inequality must lead to equality and yet never leads there. Crisis and reform are in fact the normal functioning of the system, the normal functioning of an 'equalized' inequality wherein pedagogical reason and social reason are made indistinguishable from one another.

It is indeed remarkable that this education declared unable to 'reduce' inequality presents itself more and more as an analogy to the social system. In this sense, it could be said that the jacotist analysis of pedagogical reason as a new, generalized form of inequality has been proven perfectly. Jacotot had sensed, in the role that 'progressive' people of his time had given to the people's education, the premises of a new form of the distribution of the sensible, an equivalence between pedagogical reason and social reason. He sensed this, at the heart of a society where such an equivalence was still only a utopia, where the value and steadfastness of class divisions, and of social hierarchy, was blatantly affirmed by the elites, where inequality was affirmed as the legitimate organizing principle of society. He wrote at a time when reactionaries recalled, along with their intellectual Bonald, that certain persons were 'in' society without being 'of' society, and when liberals explained through the voice of their spokesperson, minister François Guizot, that politics was a matter of 'men of leisure'. The elites of his time unabashedly professed inequality and class division. Instruction of the people was, for them, only a means of instituting certain negotiations between the top and the bottom: of giving to the poor the possibility of individual improvement and of giving to all the feeling of belonging, each in his or her own place, to the same community.

We are clearly no longer there: Our societies present themselves as homogeneous, where the lively and common pace of the multiplication of commodities and exchanges has flattened the old class divisions and has engaged all in the same pleasures and liberties. Under such conditions, the representation of inequalities tends to work more and more on the model of academic ranking: All are equal and have the potential to reach any position. No more proletariats, but only newcomers who have not yet caught up with the pace of modernity, or else the backward ones who, on the contrary, no longer succeed at keeping up with its accelerations. All are equal but certain people lack the necessary intelligence or energy to undergo the competition, or to simply follow the new exercises, that the great teacher, the grand march of Time, puts before them year after year. It is said that they do not adapt to the new technologies and mentalities, and thus flounder between the depths of class and the abyss of 'exclusion'. Society thus presents itself as a vast school, with its savages to civilize, and its problem students to put right. Under these conditions, the school is more and more charged with the fantasmatic task of filling the gap between the proclaimed equality of conditions and de facto inequality, more and more summoned to reduce inequalities that are described as merely residual.

But, the final role of this over-inflated vision of the school is, on the contrary, to reinforce the oligarchic vision of a scholarly society. Not only are state authority and economic power tied to scholarly ranking, but also the school is presented as a school without teachers, where the teachers are those at the top of the class, they are those who adapt best to progress and who show themselves capable of synthesizing scholarly concepts, concepts too complex for ordinary minds. To those who are top in their class, there is offered, afresh, the older pedagogical alternative which has become universal social logic: The austere republicans ask them to manage with the authority and distance indispensable to orderly class progression and to the interests of society; the sociologists, political scientists or journalists ask them to adapt, through dialogic pedagogy, to the modest intelligences and day-to-day problems of the less gifted, this in order to help the backward to advance, to help the excluded reintegrate themselves and to help the social fabric heal.

Expertise and journalism are the two great intellectual institutions charged with backing the government of elder statesmen, or of those first in class, by circulating, unendlessly, this new form of the social bond, this perfected explanation of inequality that structures our societies: knowledge about why those who are left behind are left behind. It is in this way, for example, that all dissenting demonstrations – from far left social movements to the extreme right wing – are, for us, a chance for intense explanatory activity on the reasons for the backwardness of archaic trade unionists, for the little savages of immigrant families, or for the middle-class families left behind by the march of progress. In good, stultifying logic, such explaining doubles as an explanation of the means by which one can extricate those left behind from their backwardness, a means unfortunately rendered ineffective by the very fact that they are left behind. Failing to lift those left behind from their backwardness, such explaining is instead perfect for solidifying the power of the advanced, which turns out to be none other than their own advancement.

This is certainly what Jacotot had in mind: the way in which the school and society symbolize each other without end, and thus endlessly reproduce the supposition of inequality, precisely by denying it. If I thought it good to revive this forgotten discourse, it is not, to repeat, in order to propose some new pedagogy. There is no jacotist pedagogy. Nor is there a jacotist anti-pedagogy, in the sense that this word is ordinarily used. In brief, jacotism is not an educational idea that one could apply to systemic school reform. The virtue of ignorance is first of all a virtue of dissociation. By asking us to dissociate teaching from knowledge, such a virtue, such a quality, precludes itself from ever being the principle of any institution where teaching and knowledge would come into harmony in order to optimize the social functioning of an institution. It is precisely against the will to harmonize, and to optimize, social functions that this critique is aimed. This critique does not forbid teaching; it does not forbid the teacher's role. It requires us instead to radically separate the ability to stand for whatever source of knowledge, and the idea of the social, global function of an institution. It requires us to separate the ability to be, for an other, the source of an enacted equality, and the idea of a social institution charged with achieving equality.

Equality, Jacotot maintains, only exists in the act, and only for individuals. It is lost as soon as it is considered collectively. It is possible to correct this verdict, to consider the possibility of collective acts of equality. But, this possibility itself presupposes that we keep separate various demonstrations of equality, that we consequently refuse the idea of institutional mediation, of social mediation, between individual demonstrations of equality and collective ones. Doubtless, individual demonstrations and collective ones have the same presupposition: the presupposition that equality is ultimately the condition of possibility of inequality itself, and that it is possible to effect this condition, this equality. There is thus an analogy between the effects of the egalitarian axiom, just as there is between the effects of the inegalitarian axiom. But the non-egalitarian analogy functions as a real social operation. It is this uninterrupted operation that Jacotot theorizes in the concept of explanation. But the same does not go for the egalitarian axiom. The act that emancipates an intelligence has, on its own, no effect on the social order. And the egalitarian axiom requires refusing the idea of such an operation. It prohibits the thought of a social logic by which individual demonstrations transform themselves into collective ones. It is indeed in this way that reasons for inequality impinge upon the reasons for equality.

The explicative-explained society, the unequal-equalized society, such a society requires the harmonization of functions. It requires of teachers in particular that we merge our competence as learned researchers, our function as teachers working in an institution, and our activity as citizens, into a single energy that advances, in one effort, knowledge transmission, social integration, and civic conscience. It is this requirement that the 'ignorant schoolmaster's' particular manner asks us to ignore. The virtue of the ignorant schoolmaster lies in knowing that a learned person is not a teacher, that a teacher is not a citizen, that a citizen is not a learned person. Not that it is impossible to be all three at once. What is impossible, instead, is to harmonize the roles of these three figures. Such harmonization only happens in the sense of the dominant explanation. The idea of emancipation demands the division of various logics. It shows us that, if we wish, it is possible to engage the social machine even as it runs, through the invention of individual and collective forms of egalitarian acts, but never to confuse these functions. It requires us to refuse to mediate equality.

Such, it seems to me, is the lesson that we draw from this particular dissonance affirmed at the very onset of the modern educational-social machine. Equality is enacted within the social machine through dissensus. And dissensus is not primarily a quarrel, but is a gap in the very configuration of sensible concepts, a dissociation introduced into the correspondence between ways of being and ways of doing, seeing and speaking. Equality is at once the final principle of all social and governmental order and the omitted cause of its 'normal' functioning. It resides neither in a system of constitutional forms nor in the form of societal mores, nor in the uniform teaching of the republic's children, nor in the availability of affordable products in supermarket displays. Equality is fundamental and absent, timely and untimely, always up to the initiative of individuals and groups who, set against the ordinary course of events, take the risk of verifying their equality, of inventing individual and collective forms for its verification. Affirmation of these simple principles in fact constitutes an unprecedented dissonance, a dissonance one must, in a way, forget

15

in order to continue improving schools, programs and pedagogies, but that one must also, from time to time, listen to again so that the act of teaching does not lose sight of the paradoxes that give it meaning.

AN AFTERWORD ON TRANSLATION

Jacques Rancière's 'On Ignorant Schoolmasters' establishes significant links between his various philosophical convictions, links that might otherwise be established only through conjecture, especially at this time in the English-speaking world when Rancière's work in still undergoing translation. These links concern education, politics, philosophy, language, intelligence, equality and freedom. A few small matters, to be sure. But while it is a common practice for an introduction to offer a précis of the work it introduces, it would be unfortunate to take the role of explicator of a text whose author has shown so plainly the stultifying results of a 'society pedagogicized', a society of teachers, or in this case translators, 'who show themselves capable of synthesizing scholarly concepts, concepts too complex for ordinary minds'.[2] Thus, no more will be said about the links that should speak for themselves in the pages that follow.

In a different, if more personal, vein, we want to point out an aspect of translating Rancière's text, an aspect that seems to graft well to the beginning of his text. Then, we will offer a thought on the current, neoliberal state of educational policy, a thought that might be inserted somewhere in the middle of 'On Ignorant Schoolmasters', at the point where Rancière addresses French educational theory in the late twentieth century. Finally, we will offer a coda that might appropriately come at the end of his text since it bears on the paradox that Rancière introduces in its last few lines, a paradox he leaves unexplored yet begging for exploration. This translator introduction will thus serve as a supplement to the text's beginning, middle and end. If it nevertheless explains something and thus stultifies in the process, it is with a translator's fumbling apology.

The Translator

Translating the work of Jacques Rancière, especially a work on ignorant schoolmasters, it is impossible not to notice a certain coincidence. The ignorant schoolmaster is, after all, none other than Joseph Jacotot, who demands of his students to translate, to translate from a language unknown to the schoolmaster into a language unknown to his students. As translator of one who has introduced this schoolmaster into the crosshairs of current educational theory, it is hard not to put oneself in the place of Jacotot's students, who were set the following task:

> He put it [a copy of *Télémaque*] in his students' hands and told them, through an interpreter, to read half of the book with the aid of the translation, to constantly repeat what they had learned, to read the other half quickly, and to write in French what they thought of it.

As translator, one joins Jacotot's students. One compares a French text with the English text under composition. One fumbles between French and English in a way that Jacotot's students must have fumbled between Flemish and French. One experiences the defamiliarization, and, yes, the exhilaration, that ensues as soon as one decides to proceed, by leap of faith, from one language to another. This leap of faith is all too familiar to one who must 'try on' a new language for the first time, whether it be 'trying on' the French language by students who have never known any French before, whether it be 'trying on' a new language when one finds oneself in a country where no one understands the words you speak, or whether it be 'trying on' a translation from one language to another in order to see if an original text speaks, in one language, the way the text speaks in another.

But, the aim here is not to show how a translator, one sanctioned by Jacques Rancière to translate 'On Ignorant Schoolmasters', is partaking in an act of intellectual emancipation akin to that of Jacotot's students. It is banal to mention that one who writes a text is probably as emancipated as the one who reads that text, banal to mention that Fénelon, who authored the bilingual *Télémaque* studied by Jacotot's students, was probably emancipated at least as much as those students whose emancipation consisted of studying that bilingual addition. It is indeed hard *not* to say that the author of a work is at least as emancipated as those who labour at understanding the work. And when such an author's work finds its way into a classroom, as the *Télémaque* found its way into Jacotot's classroom, it is rather safe to say that the author of such a piece of curriculum finds him or herself in a position at least as emancipated, if not more emancipated, than those students who are sent to study their curriculum.

In a similar way, it is not hard to say that the author of a translation such as the present one might be at least, if not more, intellectually emancipated than the ones who will rely on this very text, on such an author's work, for their own English understanding of Rancière's French words. Inconsistent with the aims of the ignorant schoolmaster, and with Rancière's text, the above scenarios actually stray from the coincidence mentioned earlier. They stray because they establish a set of hierarchies: author over reader, curriculum designer over student, translator over one who is monolingual, one scholar over another, etc.

The coincidence of translating Rancière's text and reading the *Télémaque* is instead a flat coincidence, a coincidence of equality. Its equality has two important aspects. First, translating without the stultification of a teacher is no different than translating for publication. One act is not more authoritative than the other. Both student and translator are thrown back to an originary state of language manipulation similar to the child who acquires language for the first time. The translator, the student and the infant are faced with the daunting task of communicating in a way that they have heretofore not experienced communication. They are faced with negotiating a relationship between 'seeing, saying and doing', as Rancière is so fond of putting it. The translator, in this sense, is no less obliged to struggle at his or her task than the student or the infant. All are faced with an intellectual challenge that is equal to 'the most difficult of apprenticeships: the apprenticeship of that foreign language that is, for every child arriving in the world, called his or her mother tongue'. There is no hierarchy between translator and student. Each is in the originary, and challenging, position of the 'child arriving in the world'.

In addition to the challenge shared equally by infant, student and translator, there is a parity of ambiguity. When the infant tries to use a new expression, he or she will be met with understanding or perhaps with bewilderment. From this point, the infant will con-template the results of such an attempt, will reuse the expression under slightly different circumstances, will compare and contrast and will move forward only slightly better informed than before. This trial and error demands an exhilarating experience of ambiguity, but such experience, such fumbling, is the bedrock of intellectual emancipation. The student who reads *Télémaque* experiences this ambiguity, too, even if he or she is older and already understands the mother tongue. The ignorant schoolmaster's student repeats and tests, compares and verifies, conjectures and reformulates with great tolerance for the ambiguity that must accompany any act of translation. But such a student will never be sure of accuracy; he or she will only know that communication has occurred in a way that seemed to have meaning. And this is certainly the fumbling of the academic translator. Ultimately, one never knows if one has translated 'correctly'. Not even a person perfectly fluent in the languages under translation escapes this fumbling. One only knows that one's way of translating has withstood a certain amount of trial and error. The infant, the student and the translator are equal as they undergo the trial of intellectual uncertainty.

Stultification and Neoliberalism

Towards the middle of 'On Ignorant Schoolmasters', Rancière introduces Jacotot's critique of 'society pedagogicized' to the concerns of modern-day education in France, and in doing so provides an excellent critique of critical, traditional and progressive movements in education. It is important, though, to augment Rancière's presentation since neoliberalism has become an additional condition of educational practices in many parts of the world. The following question arises: How does Rancière's preliminary work on Pierre Bourdieu, Republicanism and progressivism help us to theorize the current discourses around neoliberalism in education. Picking up where Rancière left off, one might offer the following brief analysis.

Neoliberalism in education has three major attributes: accountability, competition and privatization. These attributes are embraced to a greater or lesser extent by many educational constituencies on the assumption that student underachievement will be remedied by the magic circle connecting these three points of hope. Indeed, just as Rancière summarizes the scholarly debate over education in France in the 1960s and 1970s as a debate over equality and inequality, one might summarize educational politics of the 1990s and 2000s as the decades advocating an economic model for educational improvement. Accountability, competition and privatization have been touted as solutions over these two decades. The result has been more high-stakes testing of students, more media scrutiny of how one school (or school district) compares to another and more opportunities for schools to opt out (or be forced out) of the public system by means of charters or corporate take-over.

And, there has been an appropriate backlash against the three-pronged program of neoliberalism. Teachers and teachers' unions have bemoaned accountability, competition and privatization, first, on the grounds that these neoliberal practices undermine the sacred trust of public education. Under the pressure of neoliberal tendencies, the public school, and with it the public good of having an educational commons for developing democratic citizens, will continue to exist only as long as they come in ahead of the competition. Otherwise, the public school will be offered up to the mechanisms of profit maximization and free choice and teachers' unions have consistently criticized such an endgame. Secondly, teachers and their unions condemn neoliberal policies because such policies disable teachers from doing their jobs properly. On the way to the neoliberal endgame, the autonomy and expertise of teachers is notably assailed. For, neoliberalism's brand of accountability, modelled as it is after economic outcomes, constricts the realm of learning to that which is precisely measurable. Teachers end up teaching to standardized tests rather than focusing on the growth and individuality of each child.

Left-minded educational theorists have been quick to criticize educational neoliberalism as one more layer of ideological saturation. If the school is, as Bourdieu points out, a cog in the reproduction of class stratification, then the brash introduction of a neoliberal agenda only serves to intensify the separation of the haves from the have-nots. Neoliberalism is assailed as the most egregious of incursions into the school's domain. It is bad enough that schools valourize the cultural capital of children from elite backgrounds while de-valourizing the knowledge that other children bring to school. It is bad enough that teachers are unwitting accomplices in this educational reproduction of the status quo. It is arduous enough to unveil the altruistic rhetoric of the school, to expose the classroom as a site of class stratification and to re-educate unwitting teachers in order to effect some kind of educational equity. Enter now the neoliberal agenda with all its ruthlessness. Left-minded educational theorists have a brash new nemesis whose agenda is actually once removed from internecine educational squabbles. In earlier decades, critical, traditional and progressive theories of education clashed mostly over what would be taught in schools, and by which methods. (And of course, the left wanted schools to teach against the grain of neoliberal practices while they were still only 'out there' in the harsh world of the marketplace.) Now, the evil lurking in textbooks has come knocking on the school door, and there has been an appropriate critical response by the left.

It is hard to find a more fitting supplement to Rancière's account of educational politics in France. Rancière has pointed out that the two strains of educational thought once current in France, Republicanism and school reform, both partake in the very logic that the school uses to stultify students:

> Sociology calls this failure the 'crisis of the school' and it calls for school reform. Republicanism happily accuses reform itself of being the principal cause of the crisis. But reform and crisis can lead to the same jacotist notion: both are an explanation of school, a never-ending explanation of the reasons why inequality must lead to equality and yet never leads there.

That is to say, conservatives and liberals spend their time explaining things, like all good teachers. But explanation is precisely the social mechanism that keeps stultifying students, just as it stultifies a society at large that depends upon expert after expert for explanations that could not possibly be formulated by one person on his or her own. Explanations serve to cover up the fact that explanations are themselves the problem.

When it comes to left-oriented critiques of neoliberalism, the same phenomenon obtains. If accountability, competition and privatization are wrong, it is because accountability, competition and privatization are wrong. It is not because neoliberalism has some magical and nefarious shadow to cast on whatever institution comes under its spell. Yet, the critique of neoliberalism incessantly *explains* and *teaches* the bane of market thinking to all educators, and to all students, who will listen. As in the case of French educational politics, 'Pedagogical reason and social reason are made indistinguishable from one another'. Explanation becomes the order of the day. Critical explanation denounces not accountability, competition and privatization *per se*, but the underlying social logic of these practices which must be exposed as the enemy they are, the enemy called neoliberalism.

In a troubling reversal of roles, those who champion the neoliberal agenda are currently the reformers. It is they, the 'new conservatives', who have a theory for change in the fashion of criticalists of old. Of course, the neoliberal theory for change has nothing to do with education *per se*. Accountability, competition and privatization are themselves explanatory schemes. They explain the shape of the educational landscape rather than intervening in any way on educational practices. And in our pedagogicized society, it is no wonder that people respond so well to these explanations. People like new explanations, especially ones that claim to improve education. Following this role reversal, today's critical theory, like traditional theory of old, 'happily accuses reform itself of being the principal cause of the crisis'. Critical theory is in the unenviable position of explaining neoliberalism's faults at a distance even further removed from education than ever. Critical theory explains neoliberalism. Neoliberalism, in turn, explains education. Education itself remains as explanatory as ever, as explanatory as either one.

Paradoxes That Give Meaning to Teaching

In his final lines on ignorant schoolmasters, after establishing a wide-ranging critique of the social logic of teaching, Rancière rescinds his message somewhat, noting that the explanatory backwardness of education is

> a dissonance one must, in a way, forget in order to continue improving schools, programs, and pedagogies, but that one must also, from time to time, listen to again so that the act of teaching does not lose sight of the paradoxes that give it meaning.

This statement certainly calls for further comment. By way of finishing this introduction, and to offer a glimpse of sense to these enigmatic last lines, one can draw on Rancière's distinction between 'politics' and 'police'.

As Rancière details in a number of his works, most notably in *Disagreement* (Rancière 1999) and *Hatred of Democracy* (Rancière 2006c), what currently goes by the name of politics is not politics at all. It is policing. Politics, rightly identified, happens less frequently, only when a person or group of people gain voice in a heretofore unimaginable way. This latter form of politics cannot obtain under the calculating, participatory norms of societal or institutional programs. As Rancière puts it in *Disagreement*,

> Politics doesn't always happen – it actually happens very little or rarely. What is usually lumped together under the name of

political history or political science in fact stems more often than not from other mechanisms concerned with holding on to the exercise of majesty, the curacy of divinity, the command of armies, and the management of interests. Politics only occurs when these mechanisms are stopped in their tracks. (Rancière 1999, p. 17)

As Rancière's essay on ignorant schoolmasters makes clear, there are direct lines to be drawn between intellectual emancipation and politics on the one hand; between schooling, as it usually happens, and policing, on the other. Hence, the 'dissonance' and 'paradox' mentioned in those last few lines: Schooling as we know it is dependent upon a calculable if unnoticed absence of true education just as politics as we know it is most often dependent upon a similar absence in true politics. Education is, for the most part, part of the police rather than part of politics.

But while it is easy and provocative for Rancière to end this essay noting such a dissonance between educational emancipation and what is usually called schooling, it is required of Rancière's readers, or at least those readers who are concerned with 'improving schools, programs and pedagogies', to tease some sense out of this particular dissonance. For such teasing, it is helpful to turn to Rancière's work on politics *per se*, where he accounts for the tandem inconsistencies of politics and policing. In the political context, Rancière has indeed given sense to the above educational paradox. Noting the interaction of politics and policing, Rancière writes in *Disagreement*: 'Politics occurs when there is a place and a way for two heterogeneous processes to meet. The first is the police process in the sense we have tried to define. The second is the process of equality' (Rancière 1999, p. 30). Then going on to compare one police order, 'the Scythians' practice of gouging out their slaves' eyes', to another, 'the practices of modern information and communications strategies', he makes the following distinction:

There is a worse and a better police – the better one, incidentally, not being the one that adheres to the supposedly natural order of society or the science of legislators, but the one that all the breaking and entering perpetrated by egalitarian logic has most often jolted out of its 'natural' logic. (Rancière 1999, pp. 30–31)

In terms of improving schools, programs and pedagogies, the same sentiment might obtain. While there might not be a generalizable

Jacotist method for intellectual emancipation, while any such method might itself join the police order it aims to subvert, this is not to say that all schools, programs and pedagogies are the same. Some educational endeavours will be troubled by the presumption of equality more frequently, and some less. Improvement, in this sense, means more trouble. One can indeed improve the police order of schooling in order to foster events of intellectual emancipation, but such improvement will not happen under the register of what is usually understood as the improvement of schools, programs and pedagogies. Improvement in this sense would never consist of importing some new method for teachers to use, or some new program for schools introduce. Instead, because improvement means more trouble, improvement will happen when methods and programs get interrupted, get troubled, by students who are determined, as Rancière describes in *The Ignorant Schoolmaster,* to take their own 'orbit' about some 'truth' that is to be learned (Rancière 1991a, p. 59).

So, it can be said that there are better and worse schools just as it can be said that there are better and worse police. But the better school will not be one whose programs and policies are more effective than the programs and policies of the worse. The better school will be the one that is porous to the incursion of intellectual emancipation. Such emancipation will begin when the student decides it will begin, and it will belong only for the student, not for the school. It will not begin because of a policy or practice, but in spite of a policy or practice. A policy or practice can only set the orbit of learning *for* a student, while intellectual emancipation happens when a student sets out on an orbit that is wholly his or her own. As Rancière puts it in *The Ignorant Schoolmaster*, 'No one has a relationship to the truth if he is not on his own orbit' (Rancière 1991a, p. 59). The greatest conceit in education, then, is the one that is constantly embraced by so many who try to improve schools, programs and pedagogies. It is the conceit that there is some institutional means by which to improve education in order to emancipate students.

CHAPTER 2

A NEW LOGIC OF EMANCIPATION

Equality is not a goal that governments and societies could succeed in reaching. To pose equality as a goal is to hand it over to the pedagogues of progress, who widen endlessly the distance they promise that they will abolish. Equality is a presupposition, an initial axiom – or it is nothing.

(Rancière 2003a, p. 223)

INTRODUCTION

The work of Jacques Rancière deserves an educational point of entry. Or so this book will endeavour to prove. Rancière's work, at large, is more reliant on a certain vision of education than is commonly acknowledged. And in turn, educational thought could be more clearly informed by his particular vision. This is not to say that Rancière has not already intimated the significant links between educational thought and his political, historical and aesthetic 'interventions'.[1] Certainly, the essay 'On Ignorant Schoolmasters' does much by way of such intimation. It is rather to say that these links have themselves yet to be intervened on in a more extended manner. Indeed, it might be said that this entire book is an intervention on Rancière's 'On Ignorant Schoolmasters'. If that essay provides an account and a context for Rancière's primary book on education, *The Ignorant Schoolmaster* (Rancière 1991a), then this book, in turn, provides an account of that account. To establish such an account, we have chosen six themes – emancipation, the child, inclusion, recognition, truth and speech – the first of which we will begin to address in this chapter.

The idea of emancipation plays a central role in modern educational theories and practices. Many educators see their task not simply as that of modifying or conditioning the behaviour of their students. They want their students to become independent and autonomous, to be able to think for themselves, to make their own judgments and to draw their own conclusions. The emancipatory impetus is particularly prominent in critical traditions and approaches where the aim of education is conceived as that of emancipating students from oppressive practices and structures in the name of social justice and human freedom (see, for example, Gur Ze'ev 2005). What is needed to bring about emancipation, so educators in the critical tradition argue, is an explanation of the workings of power, as it is only when one sees and understands how power operates that it becomes possible to address its influence and, in a sense, escape from it. This is why notions like 'demystification' and 'liberation from dogmatism' play a central role in critical education (see, for example, Mollenhauer 1976, p. 67; McLaren 1997, p. 218; see also Biesta 1998; 2005). Because it is assumed that power also operates upon people's understandings of the situations they are in, there is an important strand within the critical tradition in which it is argued that emancipation can only be brought about 'from the outside', that is, from a position which, itself, is not contaminated by the workings of power. This line of thought goes back to Marxist notions of 'ideology' and 'false consciousness', and finds a more recent expression in Pierre Bourdieu's notion of 'misrecognition' (see Rancière 2003a, pp. 165–202). Hence, it becomes the task of the critical educator to make visible what is hidden for those who are the 'object' of the emancipatory endeavours of the critical educator. Similarly, the task of critical social science becomes that of making visible what is hidden from the everyday view.

Rancière has raised some important questions about the logic of this particular model of emancipation. Whereas according to this logic the explanation of how the world 'really' is leads to emancipation, Rancière has argued that instead of bringing about emancipation, this logic introduces a fundamental *dependency* into the attainment of emancipation. This is because the ones to be emancipated remain dependent upon the 'truth' or 'knowledge' revealed to them by the emancipator. The problem, as he puts it in *The Politics of Aesthetics*, is that 'where one searches for the hidden beneath the apparent, a position of mastery is established' (Rancière 2004a, p. 49). In *The Ignorant Schoolmaster* (Rancière 1991a), Rancière has shown in great detail how educational practices based on this logic of emancipation lead to 'stultification' rather than emancipation. In other work, particularly *The Philosopher and his Poor* (Rancière 2003a), he has shown that a relationship of dependency is, in a sense, constitutive of Western philosophy and social theory more generally. Rancière's contribution

26

not only lies in highlighting this contradiction within the logic of emancipation. Throughout his career, he has worked consistently on the articulation of an alternative approach – an alternative way to understand and 'do' emancipation. He has done so using a form that aims to be consistent with his ideas on emancipation in that it is a kind of writing that tries to avoid a position of mastery. Rancière has referred to this as a 'topographical' way of writing that articulates 'an egalitarian or anarchist theoretical position that does not presuppose this vertical relationship of top to bottom' (Rancière 2004a, pp. 49–50; see also Rancière 2009a).

The purpose of this chapter is to reconstruct and review Rancière's ideas on emancipation. We begin with a brief discussion of the history of the trajectory of the idea of emancipation, and we highlight the main contradictions within this trajectory. We then discuss aspects of Rancière's work that pertain to emancipation in order to show how and in what ways one might understand and 'do' emancipation differently. We do this from three angles: the angle of political theory, the angle of political practice and the angle of education.

EMANCIPATION AND ITS PREDICAMENTS

The concept of emancipation has its roots in Roman law where it referred to the freeing of a son or wife from the legal authority of the *pater familias*, the father of the family. Emancipation literally means to give away ownership (*ex*: away; *mancipum*: ownership). More broadly, it means to relinquish one's authority over someone. This implies that the 'object' of emancipation, that is, the person to be emancipated, becomes independent and free as a result of the act of emancipation. This is reflected in the legal use of the term today, where emancipation means the freeing of someone from the control of another, particularly in the form of parents relinquishing authority and control over a minor child. In the seventeenth century, emancipation became used in relation to religious toleration, in the eighteenth century in relation to the emancipation of slaves and in the nineteenth century in relation to the emancipation of women and workers.[2] The Roman use of the term already indicates the link with education, in that emancipation marks the moment when, and the process through which, the (dependent) child becomes an (independent) adult.

A decisive turn in the trajectory of the idea of emancipation was taken in the eighteenth century when emancipation became intertwined with the enlightenment and enlightenment became understood as a process of emancipation. We can see this most clearly in Immanuel Kant's essay 'What is Enlightenment?', in which he defined enlightenment as 'man's release from his self-incurred tutelage' and saw tutelage or immaturity as 'man's inability to make use of his understanding without the direction from another' (Kant 1992, p. 90). Immaturity is self-incurred, Kant wrote, 'when its cause lies not in lack of reason but in lack of resolution and courage to use it without the direction from another' (ibid.). Enlightenment thus entailed a process of becoming independent or autonomous, and for Kant this autonomy was based on the use of one's reason. Kant contributed two further ideas to this line of thinking. First of all, he argued that the 'propensity and vocation to free thinking' was not a contingent, historical possibility, but should be seen as something that was an inherent part of human nature; it was man's 'ultimate destination' and the 'aim of his existence' (Kant 1982, p. 701; our translation). To block progress in enlightenment was therefore 'a crime against human nature' (Kant 1992, p. 93). Secondly, Kant argued that in order for this 'capacity' to emerge, we need education. In his view, the human being can only become human – that is a rational autonomous being – 'through education' (Kant 1982, p. 699; our translation).

Kant's position clearly presents a set of interlocking ideas that has become central to modern educational thinking and that has had a profound impact on modern educational practice. Kant assumes that there is a fundamental difference between immature and mature beings and that this difference maps onto the distinction between childhood and adulthood. He defines maturity in terms of rationality – the (proper) use of one's reason – and sees rationality as the basis for independence and autonomy. Education is seen as the 'lever' for the transition from immaturity to maturity, which, in turn, means that education is intimately connected with the question of freedom. All this is aptly summarized in Kant's formulation of what is known in the literature as the educational paradox: 'How do I cultivate freedom through coercion?' (Kant 1982, p. 711; our translation).

Following Kant, we can trace the emergence of the notion of emancipation along two, related lines: One is educational, the other philosophical. The idea that education is not about the insertion of the individual into the existing order but entails an orientation towards autonomy and freedom played an important role in the establishment of education as an academic discipline in Germany towards the end of the nineteenth and the beginning of the twentieth century (see, for example, Tenorth 2008). It also was a central element in 'Reformpädagogik', 'New Education' and 'Progressive Education', which emerged in the first decades of the twentieth century in many countries around the world. In most cases, the argument against adaptation was expressed as an argument for the child. Many educationalists followed Rousseau's insight that adaptation to the external societal order would corrupt the child. This led to the idea, however, that a choice for the child could only mean a choice *against* society. This was further supported by theories which conceived of 'the child' as a natural category, a 'given', and not as something that had to be understood in social, historical and political terms.

Whereas the idea that education is about the emancipation of the individual child played an important role in the establishment of education as an academic discipline in its own right, the limitations of this view became painfully clear when it turned out that such an approach could easily be adopted by any ideological system, including Nazism and Fascism. This is why, after the Second World War, educationalists – first of all in Germany – began to argue that there could be no individual emancipation without wider societal transformation. This became the central tenet of critical approaches to education. In Germany, a major contribution came from Klaus Mollenhauer, whose critical-emancipatory approach drew inspiration from the (early) work of Jürgen Habermas (see Mollenhauer 1976). Two decades later, but with precursors in the writings of authors like John Dewey, George Counts and Paulo Freire, a similar body of work emerged in North America, particularly through the contributions of Michael Apple, Henry Giroux and Peter McLaren. As a critical theory of education, the emancipatory interest of critical pedagogies focuses on the analysis of oppressive structures, practices and theories. The key idea is that emancipation can be brought about if people gain an adequate insight into the power relations that constitute their situation – which is why the notion of 'demystification' plays a central role in critical pedagogies.

It is here that we can connect the trajectory of the idea of emancipation in education with wider philosophical discussions, at least to the extent to which this trajectory is part of the development of Marxism and neo-Marxist philosophy. It is, after all, a key insight of this tradition that in order to liberate ourselves from the oppressive workings of power and achieve emancipation, we first and foremost need to *expose* how power operates. What the Marxist tradition adds to this – and this, in turn, has influenced critical and emancipatory pedagogies – is the notion of *ideology*. Although the question of the exact meaning of this concept is a topic of ongoing debates (see Eagleton 2007), one of the crucial insights expressed in the concept of ideology is not only that all thought is socially determined – following Karl Marx's dictum that 'it is not the consciousness of man that determines their being but, on the contrary, their social being that determines their consciousness' (Marx, quoted in Eagleton 2007, p. 80) – but also, and more importantly, that ideology is thought 'which *denies* this determination' (ibid.: p. 89) The latter claim can be linked to Friedrich Engels's notion of false consciousness: the idea that 'the real motives impelling [the agent] remain unknown to him' (Engels, quoted in Eagleton 2007, p. 89). The predicament of ideology lies in the suggestion that it is precisely because of the way in which power works upon our consciousness, that we are unable to see how power works upon our consciousness. This not only implies that in order to free ourselves from the workings of power we need to expose how power works upon our consciousness. It also means that in order for us to achieve emancipation, *someone else*, whose consciousness is not subjected to the workings of power, needs to provide us with an account of our objective condition. According to this logic, therefore, emancipation is ultimately contingent upon the truth about our objective condition, a truth that can only be generated by someone who is positioned outside of the influence of ideology – and in the Marxist tradition this position is considered to be occupied either by science or by philosophy.

What this brief description of emancipation's philosophical and educational emergence begins to reveal are the contours of a certain 'logic' of emancipation, a certain way in which emancipation is conceived and understood. There are several aspects to this logic. One is that emancipation requires an intervention from the 'outside'; an intervention, moreover, by someone who is not subjected to the power that needs to be overcome. This not only shows that emancipation is understood as something that is *done to* somebody. It also reveals that emancipation is based upon a fundamental *inequality* between the emancipator and the one to be emancipated. Equality, on this account, becomes the outcome of emancipation; it becomes something that lies in the future. Moreover, it is this outcome which is used to legitimize the interventions of the emancipator. Whereas this view of emancipation follows more or less directly from philosophical considerations, particularly around the notion of ideology, it is not too difficult to recognize a particular pedagogy in this account as well. This is a pedagogy in which the teacher knows and students do not know *yet*; where it is the task of the teacher to explain the world to the students and where it is the task of the students to ultimately become as knowledgeable as the teacher. We can say, therefore, that the logic of emancipation is also the logic of a particular pedagogy. Although much of this will sound familiar – which, in a sense, proves how influential this modern logic of emancipation has been – this 'logic' of emancipation is not without problems or, to be more precise, it is not without contradictions.

The first contradiction is that although emancipation is orientated towards equality, independence and freedom, it actually installs *dependency* at the very heart of the 'act' of emancipation. The one to be emancipated is, after all, dependent upon the intervention of the emancipator, an intervention based upon a knowledge that is fundamentally inaccessible to the one to be emancipated. When there is no intervention, there is, therefore, no emancipation. This raises the question when this dependency will actually disappear. Is it as soon as emancipation is achieved? Or should the one who is emancipated remain eternally grateful to his or her emancipator for the 'gift' of emancipation? Should slaves remain grateful to their masters for setting them free? Should women remain grateful to men for setting them free? Should children remain grateful to their parents for setting them free? Or could all of them perhaps have asked why they were not considered to be free in the first place?

Modern emancipation is not only based upon dependency but also based upon a fundamental *inequality* between the emancipator and the one to be emancipated. According to the modern logic of emancipation, the emancipator is the one who knows better and best, and who can perform the act of demystification that is needed to expose the workings of power. According to the modern logic of emancipation, the emancipator does not simply occupy a superior position. It could even be argued that in order for this superiority to exist, the emancipator actually needs the inferiority of the one to be emancipated. Again, we can ask when this inequality will actually disappear. After all, as long as the master remains a master, the slave can only ever become a former slave or an emancipated slave – but not a master. The slave, in other words, will always lag behind in this logic of emancipation.

The third contradiction within the modern logic of emancipation has to do with the fact that although emancipation takes place in the interest of those to be emancipated, it is based upon a fundamental *distrust* of and *suspicion* about their experiences. The logic of emancipation dictates, after all, that we cannot really trust what we see or feel, and that we need someone else to tell us what it is that we are really experiencing and what our problems really are. We need someone, in other words, who 'lifts a veil off the obscurity of things', who 'carries obscure depth to the clear surface, and who, conversely, brings the false appearance of the surface back to the secret depths of reason' (Rancière, this volume, p. 4) And once more we can ask what it would mean for those 'waiting' for their emancipation to be told the 'truth' about themselves, their situation and their problems.

These contradictions not only permeate the general logic of emancipation but also are also present in the way in which this logic is manifest in a particular modern or, as Rancière has called it, a particular progressive pedagogy (Rancière 1991a, p. 121; see also Pelletier 2009). We now wish to turn to Rancière's writings in order to show how he has problematized this specific way of understanding emancipation, and how he has sought to articulate a different way for understanding and 'doing' emancipation and for posing the problem of emancipation in the first place.

EMANCIPATION, POLITICS AND DEMOCRACY

In *On the shores of politics,* Rancière characterizes 'emancipation' as 'escaping from a minority' (Rancière 1995a, p. 48). Although this could be read as a formal definition of emancipation as it refers to ending a situation in which one is a minor, the use of the word 'escape' already signals a different dynamic from the one outlined above since it associates emancipation with an activity of the one who 'achieves' emancipation rather than as something that is done *to* somebody. Rancière indeed writes that 'nobody escapes from the social minority save by their own efforts' (ibid.). Emancipation is, however, not simply about the move from a minority position to a majority position. It is not a shift in membership from a minority group to a majority group. Emancipation rather entails a 'rupture in the order of things' (Rancière 2003a, p. 219) – a rupture, moreover, that makes the appearance of subjectivity possible or, to be more precise, a rupture

that *is* the appearance of subjectivity. In this way, emancipation can
be understood as a process of *subjectification.*

Rancière defines subjectification as 'the production through a series
of actions of a body and a capacity for enunciation not previously
identifiable within a given field of experience, whose identification is
thus part of the reconfiguration of the field of experience' (Rancière
1999, p. 35; see also Rancière 1995b). There are two things that are
important in this definition, and they hang closely together. The first
thing to emphasize is the supplementary nature of subjectification
(Rancière 2003a, pp. 224–225). Subjectification, Rancière argues, is
different from identification (see Rancière 1995, p. 37). Identification
is about taking up an existing identity, that is, a way of being and
speaking and of being identifiable and visible that is already possible
within the existing order – or, to use Rancière's phrases, within the
existing 'perceptual field' or 'sensible world' (Rancière 2003a, p. 226).
Subjectification, on the other hand, is always 'disidentification,
removal from the naturalness of a place' (Rancière 1995a, p. 36).
Subjectification 'inscribes a subject name as being different from any
identified part of the community' (ibid., p. 37). When Rancière uses
the notion of 'appearance' in this context, it is not, as he puts it, to
refer to 'the illusion masking the reality of reality' (Rancière 2003a,
p. 224). Subjectification is about the appearance – the 'coming into
presence' (Biesta 2006) – of a way of being that had no place and no
part in the existing order of things. Subjectification is therefore a
supplement to the existing order because it adds something to this
order; and precisely for this reason the supplement also *divides* the
existing order, the existing 'division of the sensible' (Rancière 2003a,
pp. 224–225).[3] Subjectification thus 'redefines the field of experience
that gave to each their identity with their lot' (Rancière 1995a, p. 40).
It 'decomposes and recomposes the relationships between the ways of
doing, of *being* and of *saying* that define the perceptible organization
of the community' (ibid.).

Subjectification – and this is the second point – is therefore highly
political as it intervenes in and reconfigures the existing order of
things, the existing division or distribution of the sensible, that is, of
what is 'capable of being apprehended by the senses' (Rancière 2004a,
p. 85). As we have already seen, in order to grasp the supplementary
nature of subjectification and hence the supplementary nature of
politics itself, Rancière makes a distinction within the notion of the
political between two concepts: *police* (or police order) and *politics*.[4]

Police

Rancière defines police as 'an order of bodies that defines the alloca-
tion of ways of doing, ways of being, and ways of saying, and that sees
that those bodies are assigned by name to a particular place and task'
(Rancière 1999, p. 29). It as an order 'of the visible and the sayable that

discourse
&
noise

sees that a particular activity is visible and another is not, that this
speech is understood as discourse and another as noise' (ibid.). Police
should not be understood as the way in which the state structures the
life of society. It is not, in Habermasian terms, the 'grip' of the system
on the lifeworld (Habermas 1987), but includes *both*. As Rancière
explains, 'The distribution of places and roles that defines a police
regime stems as much from the assumed spontaneity of social relations
as from the rigidity of state functions' (Rancière 1999, p. 29). 'Policing'
is therefore not so much about 'the 'disciplining; of bodies' as it is 'a
rule governing their appearing, a configuration of *occupations* and the
properties of the spaces where these occupations are distributed' (ibid.;
emphasis in original). One way to read this definition of police is to
think of it as an order that is *all-inclusive* in that everyone has a particular place, role or position in it; that there is an identity for everyone
(we return to this in Chapter 4). This is not to say that everyone is
included in the running of the order. The point simply is that no one is
excluded from the order. After all, women, children, slaves and immigrants had a clear place in the democracy of Athens, namely, as those
who were not allowed to participate in political decision making. In
precisely this respect every police order is all-inclusive.

'Politics' then refers to 'the mode of acting that perturbs this
arrangement' (Rancière 2003a, p. 226) and that does so in the name
of, or with reference to, equality. Rancière thus reserves the term
'politics' 'for an extremely determined activity antagonistic to policing: 'whatever breaks with the tangible configuration whereby
parties and parts or lack of them are defined by a presupposition
that, by definition, has no place in that configuration' (Rancière
1999, pp. 29–30). This break is manifested as a series of actions 'that
reconfigure the space where parties, parts, or lack of parts have been
defined' (ibid., p. 30). Political activity so conceived is 'whatever shifts
a body from the place assigned to it. (. . .) It makes visible what had
no business being seen, and makes heard a discourse where once
there was only place for noise' (ibid., p. 30).

[P]olitical activity is always a mode of expression that undoes
the perceptible divisions of the police order by implementing a

basically heterogeneous assumption, that of a part of those who have no part, an assumption that, at the end of the day, itself demonstrates the sheer contingency of the order [and] the equality of any speaking being with any other speaking being. (ibid.)

Politics thus refers to the event when two 'heterogeneous processes' meet: The police process and the process of *equality* (see ibid.). The latter has to do with 'an open set of practices driven by the assumption of equality between any and every speaking being and by the concern to test this equality' (ibid.).[5]

For Rancière, politics understood in this way is always *democratic* politics. Democracy is however 'not a regime or a social way of life' – it is not and cannot be, in other words, part of the police order – but should rather be understood 'as the institution of politics itself' (ibid., p. 101). Every politics is democratic, *not* in the sense of a set of institutions, but in the sense of forms of expression 'that confront the logic of equality with the logic of the police order' (ibid.). Democracy, so we might say, is a 'claim' for equality. Democracy – or, to be more precise, the appearance of democracy – is therefore not simply the situation in which a group that has previously been excluded from the realm of politics steps forward to claim its place under the sun. It is at the very same time the *creation* of a group as a group with a particular identity that didn't exist before. Democratic activity is, for example, to be found in the activity of nineteenth-century workers 'who established a collective basis for work relations' that were previously seen as 'the product of an infinite number of relationships between private individuals' (ibid., p. 30). Democracy thus establishes new, political identities, identities that were not part of and did not exist in the existing order – and in precisely this sense it is a process of subjectification. Or as Rancière puts it: 'Democracy is the designation of subjects that do not coincide with the parties of the state or of society' (ibid., pp. 99–100).

This further means that 'the place where the people appear' is the place 'where a dispute is conducted' (ibid., p. 100). Rancière emphasizes that this dispute – which is the proper 'form' of democracy – 'is not the opposition of interests or opinions between social parties' (Rancière 2003a, p. 225). Democracy, he explains,

is neither the consultation of the various parties of society concerning their respective interests, nor the common law that imposes itself equally on everyone. The demos that gives it its name is neither the ideal people of sovereignty, nor the sum of the parties of society, nor even the poor and suffering sector of this society. (ibid.)

The political dispute rather is a conflict 'over the very count of those parties' (Rancière 1999, p. 100). It is a dispute between 'the police logic of the distribution of places and the political logic of the egalitarian act' (ibid.). Politics is therefore 'primarily a conflict over the existence of a common stage and over the existence and status of those present on it' (ibid., pp. 26–27). The essence of democracy/politics therefore is dissensus rather than consensus (see Rancière 2003a, p. 226). But, dissensus is not the 'opposition of interests or opinions. It is the production, within a determined, sensible world, of a given that is heterogeneous to it' (ibid.). In precisely this sense we could say, therefore, that politics is productive or poetic in that it generates subjectivity rather than that it depends on a particular kind of political subjectivity. This, however, is not about creating 'subjects ex nihilo' – politics, as a 'mode of subjectification' creates subjects 'by transforming identities defined in the natural order' (Rancière 1999, p. 36). It is in this sense that Rancière argues that politics is aesthetics 'in that it makes visible what had been excluded from a perceptual field, and in that it makes audible what used to be inaudible' (ibid.). This is also why Rancière emphasizes that a political subject 'is not a group that "becomes aware" of itself, finds its voice, imposes its weight on society', because establishing oneself as a subject does not happen before the 'act' of politics but rather in and through it (ibid., p. 40). Rancière characterizes a political subject as

an operator that connects and disconnects different areas, regions, identities, functions, and capacities existing in the configuration of a given experience – that is, in the nexus of distributions of the police order and whatever equality is already inscribed there, however fragile and fleeting such inscriptions may be. (ibid.)

Rancière gives the example of Jeanne Deroin who, in 1849, presents herself as a candidate for a legislative election in which she cannot run. Through this 'she demonstrates the contradiction within a universal suffrage that excludes her sex from any such universality' (ibid., p. 41). It is the staging 'of the very contradiction between police logic and political logic' (ibid.) that makes this into a political act. It is the 'bringing into relationship of two unconnected things [that] becomes the measure of what is incommensurable between two orders' and this produces both 'new inscriptions of equality within liberty and a fresh sphere of visibility for further demonstrations'(ibid., p. 42). This is why for Rancière politics is not made up of power relationships but of 'relationships between worlds' (ibid.).

It is important to see that for Rancière the point of politics is not to create constant chaos and disruption. Although Rancière would maintain that politics is basically a good thing, this does not mean that the police order is necessarily bad. Although this may not be very prominent in Rancière's work – which means that it is easily overlooked – he does argue that democratic disputes can have a positive effect on the police order in that they produce 'inscriptions of equality' (ibid.) – they leave traces behind in the (transformed) police order. This is why Rancière emphasizes that '(t)here is a worse and a better police' (ibid., pp. 30–31). The better one is, however, not the one 'that adheres to the supposedly natural order of society or the science of legislators' – it is the one 'that all the breaking and entering perpetrated by egalitarian logic has most jolted out of its 'natural' logic' (ibid., p. 31) Rancière thus acknowledges that the police 'can produce all sorts of good, and one kind of police may be infinitely preferable to another' (ibid.) But whether the police order is 'sweet and kind' does not make it any less the opposite of politics. This also means that for Rancière politics is quite rare – or as he puts it in *On the shores of politics*: politics, and hence democracy can only ever be 'sporadic' (Rancière 1995a, p. 41). As politics consists in the interruption of the police order, it can never become that order itself. Politics 'is always local and occasional' which is why its 'actual eclipse is perfectly real and no political science exists that could map its future any more than a political ethics that would make its existence the object solely of will' (Rancière 1999, p. 139).

It is not difficult to see that the idea of equality permeates everything that Rancière has to say about politics, democracy and emancipation. In fact, later we will demonstrate an *educational* understanding of equality wherein equality can be understood through the linguistic practices of children. But what is, for the moment, most significant about Rancière's position is that he does not conceive of equality as something that has to be achieved through politics. For Rancière, democracy doesn't denote a situation in which we all have become equals, nor is emancipation the process where we move from inequality to equality, that is, a process through which we overcome inequality and become equals. For Rancière, equality is not a goal that needs to be achieved through political or other means. Equality, as he puts it, 'is a presupposition, an initial axiom – or it is nothing' (Rancière 2003a, p. 223). What we can do – and what, in a sense, drives politics or makes something political – is to test or verify the assumption of equality in concrete situations. Rancière explains that what makes an action political 'is not its object or the place where it is carried out, but solely its form, the form in which confirmation of equality is inscribed in the setting up of a dispute, of a community existing solely though being divided' (Rancière 1999, p. 32). For a thing to be political, therefore, 'it must give rise to a meeting of police logic and egalitarian logic that is never set up in advance' (ibid.). This means that nothing is political in itself. But anything may become political 'if it gives rise to a meeting of these two logics' (ibid.). Equality is therefore not a principle that politics needs to press into service. 'It is a mere assumption that needs to be discerned within the practices implementing it' (ibid., p. 33). Yet, equality only generates politics 'when it is implemented in the specific form of a particular case of dissensus' (Rancière 2004a, p. 52) and it is then that 'a specific subject is constituted, a supernumerary subject in relation to the calculated number of groups, places, and functions of society' (ibid., p. 51).

THE PRACTICE OF EMANCIPATION

If traditional emancipation starts from the assumption of inequality and sees emancipation as the act through which someone is made equal through an intervention from the outside, Rancière conceives of emancipation as something that people do for themselves. For this, they do not have to wait until someone explains their objective condition to them. Emancipation 'simply' means to act on the basis of the presupposition – or 'axiom' – of equality. In this sense, it is a kind of 'testing of equality' (Rancière 1995a, p. 45). More than a reversal of the traditional way to understand emancipation – which would still accept the legitimacy of the way in which the problem that emancipation needs to resolve is formulated, that is that it starts from inequality that needs to be overcome – Rancière displaces the 'vocabulary' of emancipation and suggests new questions as much as new answers.

The thesis he puts forward in his book *The Nights of Labor* (Rancière 1991b) is that working-class emancipation was neither about the importation of scientific thought – i.e., knowledge about their objective condition – into the worker's world, nor about the affirmation of a worker culture. It rather was 'a rupture in the traditional division [*partage*] assigning the privilege of thought to some and the tasks of production to others' (Rancière 2003a, p. 219). Rancière thus showed that the French workers 'who, in the nineteenth century, created newspapers or associations, wrote poems, or joined utopian groups were claiming the status of fully speaking and thinking beings' (ibid.). Their emancipation was thus based on 'the transgressive will . . . to act as if intellectual equality were indeed real and effectual' (ibid.). Rancière argues that what the workers did was different from how emancipation is traditionally conceived. He explains this in terms of the 'syllogism of emancipation' (Rancière 1995a, p. 45). The major premise of the syllogism is that 'all French people are equal before the law' (ibid.). The minor premise is derived from direct experience, for example the fact that tailors in Paris went on strike because they were not treated as equals with regard to their pay. There is, therefore, a real contradiction. But, as Rancière argues, there are two ways in which this contradiction can be conceived. The first is the way 'to which we are accustomed' which says 'that the legal/political words are illusory, that the equality asserted is merely a façade designed to mask the reality of inequality' (ibid., p. 46). 'Thus reasons the good sense of demystification'. (ibid., p. 47) The workers, however, took the other option by taking the major premise seriously. The tailors' strike of 1833 thus took the form of a logical proof. And what had to be demonstrated through their strike was precisely equality.

Writing about this event Rancière observes that one of the demands of the tailors 'seemed strange' as it was a request for " 'relations of equality" with the masters' (ibid., pp. 47–48). What they did through this was not denying or trying to overcome the relation of economic dependence that existed between them and their masters. Yet, by making a claim to a different kind of relationship, a relationship of legal equality – by confronting the world of economic inequality with the world of legal equality – they engendered, as Rancière puts it, 'a different social reality, one founded on equality' (ibid., p. 48). What is important here – and this is the reason we focus on the detail of the example – is that emancipation in this case was not about overcoming the economic inequality but consisted in establishing a new social relationship, in this case one in which negotiation between workers and their masters became a customary element of their relationship. Rancière summarizes what was at stake here as follows:

> This social equality is neither a simple legal/political equality nor an economic levelling. It is an equality enshrined as a potentiality in legal/political texts, then translated, displaced and maximized in everyday life. Nor is it the whole of equality: it is a way of living out the relation between equality and inequality, of living it and at the same time displacing it in a positive way. (ibid.)

Emancipation here is therefore not a matter of 'making labour the founding principle of the new society'. It rather is about the workers emerging from their minority status 'and proving that they truly belong to the society, that they truly communicate with all in a common space' (ibid.). They prove through their actions, in other words, 'that they are not merely creatures of need, of complaint and protests, but creatures of discourse and reason, that they are capable of opposing reason with reason and of giving their action a demonstrative form' (ibid.). 'Self-emancipation', as Rancière calls it in this context, is therefore 'self-affirmation as a joint-sharer in a common world' (ibid., p. 49). Rancière adds that 'proving one is correct has never compelled others to recognize they are wrong' (ibid.). This is why the 'space of shared meaning' is not a space of consensus but of dissensus and transgression. It is a 'forced entry' into a common world. This not only means that the call for equality 'never makes itself heard without defining its own space' (ibid., p. 50), it also means that this call for equality must be articulated 'as though the other can always understand [one's] arguments' (ibid.). Rancière warns that those who on general grounds say that the other cannot understand them, that there is no common language, 'lose any basis for rights of their own to be recognized' (ibid.). This is why the 'narrow path of emancipation' passes between the 'acceptance of separate worlds' and the 'illusion of consensus' – but it is neither of these options.

Rancière concludes that at the heart of this 'new idea of emancipation' thus lies a notion of 'equality of intelligences as the common prerequisite of both intelligibility and community, as a presupposition which everyone must strive to validate on their own account' (ibid., p. 51). The 'democratic man' – the political subject or subject of politics – is therefore 'a being who speaks', and in this regard, it is a 'poetic being' (ibid., p. 51). This democratic human being, Rancière adds, is capable of embracing 'a distance between words and things which is not deception, not trickery, but humanity' (ibid.). The democratic human being is capable of embracing what Rancière refers to as 'the unreality of representation' by which he means the unreality of the idea of equality as well as the arbitrary nature of language. But to say that equality is not real doesn't mean that it is an illusion – and precisely here Rancière articulates a position that no longer relies on the need for demystification. He argues that we must start from equality – 'asserting equality, assuming equality as a given, working out from equality, trying to work out how productive it can be' – in order to maximize 'all possible liberty and equality' (ibid., pp. 51–52). The one who doesn't start from here but instead starts out from distrust, and 'who assumes inequality and proposes to reduce it' can only succeed in setting up 'a hierarchy of inequalities . . . and will produce inequality ad infinitum' (ibid., p. 52).

EDUCATION AND EMANCIPATION

The question whether we should start from the assumption of equality or inequality is not only a question for politics but also a central question for education, particularly given the prominent role of education and a kind of pedagogical thinking more generally, in the Enlightenment 'project' of emancipation. One might even argue that the 'pedagogy' of traditional emancipation is identical to the pedagogy of traditional education, in that education is often conceived as a practice in which those who do not yet know receive knowledge from those who do know (and are thus dependent upon those who know for their trajectory towards equality and emancipation). Education so conceived thus starts from a fundamental inequality between the one who educates and the one who receives – and needs – education. The question for Rancière is whether this is the only way in which we can understand the logic of education – and hence the logic of emancipation. In *The Ignorant Schoolmaster* Jacotot doesn't conceive of education as a process that starts from inequality in order to bring about equality, but rather conceives of education based on the fundamental assumption of the equality of intelligence of all human beings.

Jacotot's method, as we have seen, was based on the discovery he made when he was asked to teach students whose language he didn't speak. The success of his endeavours taught him that what he had always thought of as being essential for education – explication – was actually not necessary in order for his students to learn. Jacotot thus began to see that explication, rather than being the core of educational activity, actually renders students stupid since to explain something to someone 'is first of all to show him he cannot understand it by himself' (Rancière 1991a, p. 6). Explanation is therefore the 'myth of pedagogy, the parable of a world divided into knowing minds and ignorant ones' (ibid.). The explicator's 'special trick' consists of a 'double inaugural gesture' where 'he decrees the absolute beginning: it is only now that the act of learning will begin', and, 'having thrown a veil of ignorance over everything that is to be learned, he appoints himself to the task of lifting it' (ibid., pp. 6–7). The pedagogical myth thus divides the world into two and it divides intelligence into two: 'an inferior intelligence and a superior one'. Explication, from this point of view, then becomes 'enforced stultification' (ibid., p. 7).

Whereas Jacotot didn't teach his students anything – what they learned they learned through their own engagement with materials such as books – this didn't mean that they learned without a master; they only learned without a 'master explicator' (ibid., p. 12). While 'Jacotot had taught them something, he had communicated nothing to them' (ibid., p. 13). What Jacotot had done was to summon his students to use their intelligence in a 'relationship of will to will' (ibid.) Whereas explication takes place 'whenever one intelligence is subordinated to another', emancipation takes place when an intelligence obeys only itself 'even while the will obeys another will' (ibid.). From this perspective, the main educational 'problem' becomes that of revealing 'an intelligence to itself' (ibid., p. 28). What this requires is not explication but attention, that is, making the effort to use one's intelligence. As Rancière writes, what is needed is an 'absolute attention for seeing and seeing again, saying and repeating' (ibid., p. 23). The route that students will take in response to this is unknown, but what the student cannot escape, Rancière argues, is 'the exercise of his liberty' and this is summoned by a three-part question 'What do you see? What do you think about it? What do you make of it? And so on, to infinity' (ibid., see also Chapter 6 in this book).

There are therefore in Jacotot's method only two 'fundamental acts' for the master: 'He *interrogates*, he demands speech, that is to say, the manifestation of an intelligence that wasn't aware of itself or that had given up' and 'he *verifies* that the work of the intelligence is done with attention' (ibid., p. 29). Rancière emphasizes that the interrogation should not be understood in the Socratic way where the sole purpose of interrogation is to lead the student to a point that is already known by the master. What is important here is that while learning that is already known to the master 'may be the path to learning', it is 'in no way a path to emancipation' (ibid.). Central to emancipation in education, therefore, is the consciousness 'of what an intelligence can do when it considers itself equal to any other and considers any other equal to itself' (ibid., p. 39). And this is what constantly needs to be verified, namely 'the principle of the equality of all speaking beings' (ibid.). What needs to be verified is the belief that 'there is no hierarchy of *intellectual capacity*' but only 'inequality in the *manifestations* of intelligence' (ibid., p. 27). Emancipation is therefore not something '*given* by scholars, by their explications *at the level of* the people's intelligence' – emancipation is always 'emancipation seized, even against the scholars, when one teaches oneself' (ibid., p. 99). The only thing that is needed here is to summon other people to use their intelligence which means to verify 'the principle of the equality of all speaking beings' (ibid., p. 39). After all, '(w)hat stultifies the common people is not the lack of instruction, but the belief in the inferiority of their intelligence' (ibid.). The only thing that is needed is to remind people that they can see and think for themselves and are not dependent upon others who see and think for them.

Would this imply that emancipation depends on the 'truth' of the proposition that all intelligence is equal? This is not how Rancière sees it. For him, the task is to see 'what can be done under that supposition' (ibid., p. 46). As we have seen, one thing that cannot be done under this supposition is to make emancipation into a social method. Rancière insists that 'only a man can emancipate a man' (ibid., p. 102). There are 'a hundred ways to instruct, and learning also takes place at the stultifiers' school' (ibid.) – but emancipation is not about learning. Emancipation is about using one's intelligence under the assumption of the equality of intelligence. There is, therefore, 'only one way to emancipate' and to this Rancière adds that 'no party or government, no army, school, or institution, will ever emancipate a single person' (ibid.) because every institution is always a 'dramatisation' or 'embodiment' of inequality (ibid., p. 105). 'Universal teaching' – the teaching that makes emancipation possible because it starts from the assumption of equality – can therefore 'only be directed to individuals, never to societies' (ibid.)– and in the final chapter of *The ignorant schoolmaster* Rancière recounts how all attempts to turn universal teaching into a method and to institutionalize it, failed from the point of view of emancipation.

Rancière is particularly suspicious of attempts to use education – or to be more precise: schools and schooling – to bring about equality. This is of course the ambition of the 'progressives' who want to 'liberate minds and promote the abilities of the masses' (ibid., p. 121). But the idea of progress so conceived is based on what Rancière refers to as 'the pedagogical fiction', which is 'the representation of inequality as a *retard* in one's development' (ibid., p. 119). This puts the educator in the position of always being ahead of the one who needs to be educated in order to be liberated. Rancière warns, however, that as soon as we embark upon such a trajectory – a trajectory that starts from the assumption of inequality – we will never be able to reach equality. 'Never will the student catch up with the master, nor the people with its enlightened elite; but the hope of getting there makes them advance along the good road, the one of perfected explications (ibid., p. 120). The 'progressives' wish to bring about equality through 'a well-ordered system of public instruction' (ibid., p. 121). Rancière shows how Jacotot's method could even be incorporated in such a system – and actually was adopted in this way, albeit 'except in one or two small matters, namely, that the teachers using Jacotot's method were no longer teaching what they didn't know and were no longer starting from the assumption of the equality of intelligence (see ibid., p. 123). But these 'small matters' are of course crucial. The choice, therefore, is between 'making an unequal society out of equal men and making an equal society out of unequal men' (ibid., 133), and for Rancière the choice is clear. 'One only need to learn how to be equal men in an unequal society' as this is what '*being emancipated*' means (ibid.). But this 'very simple thing' is actually 'the hardest to understand' because 'the new explication – progress – has inextricably confused equality with its opposite' (ibid.) Rancière thus concludes:

> The task to which the republican hearts and minds are devoted is to make an equal society out of unequal men, to *reduce* inequality indefinitely. But whoever takes this position has only one way of carrying it through to the end, and that is the integral pedagogicization of society – the general infantilization of the individuals that make it up. Later on this will be called continuing education, that is to say, the coextension of the explicatory institutions with society. (ibid.)

EMANCIPATION AND THE INSTITUTION OF THE SCHOOL

In the preceding sections, we have reconstructed Rancière's ideas on emancipation from three different angles: the angle of political theory, the angle of political practice and the angle of education. Whereas the three accounts differ in emphasis, context and, to a certain extent, vocabulary, it is not too difficult to see the common set of ideas that runs through them, nor is it to discern the underlying 'commitment' that informs Rancière's writing. This is not to suggest that it is easy to give a name to this commitment. What emerges from Rancière's work is a commitment to a cluster of interlocking concepts: equality, democracy, emancipation. But the significance of Rancière's work does not lie in a commitment to this set of concepts *per se*, not in the least because Rancière's 'discussion partners' – if this is an appropriate expression[6] – are committed to the very same set of concepts. The ingenuity of Rancière's work lies first and foremost in the fact that he is able to show that what is done under and in the name of equality, democracy and emancipation often results in its opposite in that it reproduces inequality and keeps people in their place. What matters, therefore, is not *that* we are committed to equality, democracy and emancipation, but *how* we are committed to it and *how* we express and articulate this commitment. Rancière thus introduces a critical difference within the discourse on emancipation, equality and democracy.

One of Rancière's central insights is that as long as we project equality into the future and see it as something that has to be brought about through particular interventions and activities that aim to overcome existing inequality – such as the education of the masses or the integral pedagogicization of society – we will never reach equality but will simply reproduce inequality. The way out of this predicament is to bring equality into the here and now and act on the basis of the assumption of the equality of all human beings or, as Rancière specifies in the *Ignorant Schoolmaster*, the equality of intelligence of all human beings. To act on the basis of this assumption requires a constant verification of it – not in order to check whether the assumption *is* true *in abstracto*, but in order to *practise* the truth of the assumption, that is, to *make* it true in always concrete situations. As Rancière puts it in the *Ignorant Schoolmaster*, the problem is not to prove or disprove that all intelligence is equal, but to see 'what can be done under that supposition'. The name of the practice of the verification of the supposition of equality is 'politics'. Politics is therefore neither the practice that brings about or produces equality nor equality the principle that needs to be advanced through the activity of politics. What makes an act political is when it 'stages' the contradiction between the logic of the police order and the logic of equality, that is, when it brings into a relationship two unconnected, heterogeneous and incommensurable worlds: the police order and equality. This is why dissensus lies at the heart of political acts. Dissensus, however, should not be understood as a conflict or 'a quarrel' (Rancière, this volume, p. 15) – as that would assume that the parties involved in the conflict would already exist and have an identity. Dissensus is 'a gap in the very configuration of sensible concepts, a dissociation introduced into the correspondence between ways of being and ways of doing, seeing and speaking' (ibid.)

> Equality is at one the final principle of all social and governmental order and the omitted cause of its 'normal' functioning. It resides neither in a system of constitutional forms nor in the form of societal mores, nor in the uniform teaching of the republic's children, nor in the availability of affordable products in supermarket displays. Equality is fundamental and absent, timely and untimely, always up to the initiative of individuals and groups who (. . .) take the risk of verifying their equality, of inventing individual and collective forms for its verification. (ibid.)

This is also why the political act is an act of 'supplementary subjects inscribed as surplus in relation to any count of the parts of a society' (Rancière 2001). The political subject – which for Rancière is always also the democratic subject, the *demos* – is therefore constituted in and through the political act which is why Rancière argues that politics is a process of subjectification. We might say, therefore, that Rancière's central concepts – equality, democracy and politics – all map onto each other in that the political act consists of the verification of equality and when we do this through the staging of dissensus, democracy 'takes place', not as a political regime but as an interruption of the police order. This is also true for the notion of 'emancipation' because to *be* emancipated means to act on the basis of the assumption of equality. This has the character of a 'forced entry' into a common world which, as we have shown, not only means that the call for equality can only make itself heard by defining its own space, but must also proceed on the assumption that the other can always understand one's arguments. Emancipation therefore doesn't appear as the outcome of a particular educational trajectory. Emancipation is about using one's intelligence under the assumption of the equality of intelligence.

What is important about Rancière's thought is not only that he presents us with an account of emancipation that is radically different from the traditional account that we have outlined above. The importance of Rancière's contribution does not only lie in the fact that he helps us understand emancipation differently. His approach is also able to overcome the main contradictions within the traditional way to understand and 'do' emancipation in that for Rancière emancipation is not based upon a fundamental dependency. Nor for Rancière is emancipation based upon a fundamental inequality concealed under the aim of equality. Rancière's understanding is also no longer based upon a fundamental distrust in the experiences of the one to be emancipated to the extent that emancipation can only occur if the experiences of the one to be emancipated are replaced by a proper and correct understanding. This is not to suggest that there is no learning to be done, that there are no lessons to be learned from history and social analysis. But this learning should not be seen as dependent upon explication; it should not be staged in terms of the 'myth of pedagogy' in which the world is divided into knowing minds (emancipators/explicators) and ignorant ones. The difference here – and this is important in order to appreciate the difference Rancière aims to articulate in our understanding of the practice of emancipatory education – is not that between learning with a master and learning without a master (we return to this point in the chapters that follow). The difference is between learning with a 'master explicator' and learning without a 'master explicator'. What Rancière is hinting at, in other words, is not a school without teachers, a school without schoolmasters (see also Pelletier 2009); what he sees as the main obstacle to emancipation is the position of the 'master explicator'. There is, therefore, still authority within emancipatory education but this authority is not based on a difference of knowledge or insight or understanding. '(T)he ignorant schoolmaster exercises no relation of intelligence to intelligence. He or she is only an authority, only a will that sets the ignorant person down a path, that is to say to instigate a capacity already possessed' (Rancière, this volume, pp. 2–3).

And all this is not only an issue for the school. It is at the very same time, and perhaps first of all, an issue for society and the way in which we conceive of emancipation at large. Rancière's ideas imply a critique of a particular 'logic' of emancipation in which it is assumed that emancipation requires explanation. In this regard, we might say that Rancière's critique is aimed at any situation in which explanation emerges as the key to emancipation – the school is one example of this, but this particular 'logic' of schooling can happen in many other places too, even to the extent to which society itself becomes modelled on the explanatory logic of schooling. In this way, Rancière's critique is first and foremost a critique of a particular logic of emancipation, a logic exemplified in a particular notion of schooling but not confined to the institution of the school.

CHAPTER 3

THE FIGURE OF THE CHILD IN JACQUES RANCIÈRE AND PAULO FREIRE

Here is an anecdote that will serve as a backdrop for the discussion of childhood that follows. This is the story of a child, the sort of child Jacques Rancière posits in his writings. It is the story of a child who is learning language, and who is also becoming a political actor, as these two endeavours can be understood as one in the same. Let us call this child Barbara. She is 17 months old. Barbara is just beginning to learn language. She is just beginning to insert herself into the 'forest of signs'.[1] Barbara knows seven words so far: dada, lola, mama, nana, mulner, no and nemo. It is difficult to know whether these words should actually be written down. Certainly, their spelling can only be an adult's projection, for Barbara cannot yet write. It is doubtful whether she knows that the words she speaks have a written corollary. Nevertheless, we invent their spelling here but even our own projections are difficult to render. One cannot, for example, be sure whether these words need to be capitalized. Sometimes, they seem like proper nouns, but sometimes they do not.

Barbara uses 'dada' as might be expected. She uses it when she is reminded of her father. She never uses 'dada' when she is in her father's presence, though. She only uses the word to conjure him up when she is away from him. Her use of 'dada' is so far very limited. She will say 'dada' when her mother puts her ear to the phone and she hears her father's voice on the other end. She will repeat the word 'dada' if her mother says, 'Here comes dada, he's coming home'. 'Dada, Dada'! she will respond. These are the limits of her use of 'dada'.

'Lola' is her word of choice. It is a word that often brings a smile to Barbara's face. Lola is the family dog and she recognizes the fact that 'lola' is the dog's name. If she is putting out food for Lola, she will say 'lola' and she will look at the dog, hoping that the dog will come to where she has put the food. Barbara also uses 'lola' to designate any other dog that she sees. If she sees a dog on the street, in a book,on television or in a movie, she will yell, 'lola!' Usually, she gets the following response from whatever adult she is with: 'Yes, that is another lola-dog'. 'Lola' gets used quite often, though, because Barbara also designates any large animal as a 'lola'. Thus, with the attentive eye of a child who is learning language, 'lola's appear incessantly.

'Mama' is used to indicate Barbara's mother. She uses the word more often 'dada', but less often than 'lola'. Unlike her use of 'dada', Barbara will use 'mama' even if her mother is in her presence. That is to say, if she wants her mother to pick her up, she will say 'mama'. In contrast, if she wants her father to pick her up, she will hold up her arms and grunt. Otherwise, she uses 'mama' in a way that mirrors her use of 'dada'.

'Nana' is an especially interesting word in Barbara's vocabulary. At least her parents think it is interesting. Whether Barbara thinks it is interesting one will never know. For, 'nana' means Barbara's bottle. However, the word 'nana' seems to have no correlation to any particular word in English, proper or otherwise. 'Nana' is arbitrary. Barbara seems to have inserted the word all by herself into the English language. One day, she said 'nana' when she was upset. Her father tried to guess the reason she was so upset. He tried to pick her up and hold her. This did not make her happy either. He tried to read her a book. This did not make her happy. He tried to play 'this little piggy' with her. Still Barbara was not happy. She continued to cry and to say 'nana'. Finally, her father went to the refrigerator for milk in a baby bottle. 'Nana'? he said. Barbara smiled, took the bottle, and said 'nana'. Whenever Barbara's parents hear 'nana', they now know how to respond. Barbara uses two versions of 'nana': one with an accent on the first syllable and one with an accent on the second. The first is used when she wants her bottle. The second is used when the contents of her bottle are not to her liking.

'Mulner' is Barbara's way of pronouncing Mulder, which is the name of the family cat. Her use of 'mulner' is much the same as her use of 'lola' insofar as 'mulner' means both the family cat and any other animal she sees that is approximately the size of Mulder. There are more limits to the animals Barbara will liken to 'mulner', though, than the animals she will liken to 'lola'. For example, a rabbit elicits a cry of 'mulner', while a squirrel does not.

As many children do, Barbara uses the word 'no'. For Barbara, 'no' means 'no', but it also means 'yes'. Freud would no doubt have something to say about this. 'No' is truly a floating signifier. If asked, for example, 'Do you want to feed Lola'? Barbara will immediately reply, 'No'. Nevertheless, she *does* want to feed Lola. She will do so happily.

Barbara's final word is 'nemo'. Nemo is the name of a fish in the movie *Finding Nemo*, a movie she has watched many times. Barbara yells 'nemo' not only in the pet store when she sees a live fish. With the attentive mind of one learning through 'the most difficult of apprenticeships' (Rancière, this volume, p. 3), one hears the ubiquitous yell of 'nemo' in all sorts of places. In a bank, in a bus, on a road or wherever, if one hears 'nemo', there is sure to be a fish, or at least the representation of a fish.

It is also helpful to note Barbara's abilities that many might consider outside of language. Barbara has attained a sophisticated ability to grunt her needs and intentions, using her finger as a guide to supplement her grunting. The flexibility of this raw sign, the grunt, has too many applications to go into here. She can satisfy many of her communicative needs by grunting grunts. And of course, she babbles a lot. Her babbling happens when she is playing by herself and it is not understandable even to her parents. And finally, it should be added that Barbara's linguistic *understanding* can in no way be summarized by stating that she uses these and those words. Her understanding is very wide, but impossible to guess. Often times, her father asks her to do simple tasks that, to his knowledge, she has never heard of before. For the most part, she responds in silence, completing the task.

EDUCATIONAL INTERVENTIONS

The intention of this book is, in part, to demonstrate that Rancière's educational thought is in fact central to the numerous uses one can make of his thought in other arenas. That is to say, if one thinks *educationally* about Rancière's work, one gains great insight. To this end, we began by contextualizing the educational discourses that have gone hand in hand with the concept of emancipation, and we looked at how the education/emancipation nexus can be informed by Rancière work. One could have chosen to analyze Rancière's conceptions of emancipation and subjectification *per se*, without any reference to education, but we find such a conceptual analysis lacking. In fact, this sort of conceptual lack can best be described in terms that Rancière has already laid out quite plainly in a number of ways, one example being his treatment of political philosophy. For Rancière, political philosophy is, at its core, a contradiction in terms. This contradiction arises because politics is always sporadic and unanticipatable. It is an incursion onto the distribution of the sensible, initiated by one who is relegated to the status of noisemaker. It is instigated through a tort and practised as a demonstration of equality.[2] As such, politics cannot actually be theorized conceptually since politics always happens in particular instances, through particular acts, and in ways that are more of the essence of poetry than of the essence of theory. This is why political philosophy is a contradiction in terms. This is why 'what is called "political philosophy" might well be the set of reflective operations whereby philosophy tries to rid itself of politics, to suppress a scandal in thinking proper to the exercise of politics' (Rancière 1999, p. 12). Philosophy, as it has been applied to politics, has always attempted to conceptualize politics, and, as such, has killed politics. Politics cannot itself be conceptualized without being freeze-framed into something that is no longer politics.[3] Politics cannot be conceptualized without being hollowed out.

One might say the same of educational philosophy. If one takes education in the emancipatory sense, we have described in the previous chapter, in the sense of educational subjectification, then the venerable tradition of describing what education should do for children as they pass on towards adulthood, this venerable tradition starting with Plato's *Republic*, is contradictory in the same way that political philosophy is contradictory. This is to say, the great programs of education – in Plato, Kant, Rousseau, Spencer and, in our own times, John Dewey and Paulo Freire – these educational philosophies kill education in the same way that philosophy kills politics. As a practice of subjectification, educational emancipation, like politics, happens in ways that one cannot anticipate, in ways that cannot be anticipatable, in ways that, in short, cannot be conceptualized. As a practice of subjectification, educational emancipation begins not through the conceptual preparedness of the educator, but rather through the efforts of the student to verify his or her equality through intellectual apprehension.[4] The teacher cannot know how the student will learn, nor what the student will learn, because the student will learn something, and will learn somehow, both the something and the somehow being specific to the particular event under verification. As Rancière notes, speaking of the ignorant schoolmaster, 'The student learns something as an effect of his master's mastery, but he does not learn his master's knowledge' (Rancière 2007a). Of course, these very comments that we have made above – on the contradictions of political philosophy, and the contradictions of educational philosophy – themselves become too conceptual all too quickly. They *become* political philosophy and educational philosophy when they remain ungrounded and conceptual. They become hollow rather than educational. How does one, then, perform something other than a conceptual analysis? In this book, we are attempting to do so by turning to education as a tool for provoking Rancière's thought. But how does this provoke something other than the conceptual?

By way of performing an answer to this question and by way of bringing in an educational concern that has been overlooked by commentators on Rancière's writings, one can turn to the figure of the child in Rancière. With the figure of the child in mind, it is indeed curious that so much attention has been given recently to Rancière's conception of equality, while attention has not focused on his figure of the child. It is not curious in the sense that Rancière does not pay attention to equality. As Kristin Ross rightly notes in her introduction to *The Ignorant Schoolmaster*,

> *The Ignorant Schoolmaster* forces us to confront what any number of nihilistic, neo-liberal philosophies would have us avoid: the founding term of our political modernity, *equality*. And in the face of systematic attacks on the very idea, powerful ideologies that would relegate it to the dustbin of history or to some dimly radiant future, Rancière places equality – virtually – in the present. (Rancière 1991a, p. xxiii)

This is indeed true. Equality is central to his work on political emancipation and it is central to his work on emancipatory pedagogy. It is curious, rather, in the sense that equality, at least the presumed equality of intellectual capacity, is established in a particular way. Equality is established on an assumption about what it means for a child to learn his or her mother tongue. A child learning, a child learning his or her mother tongue – this is an educational concern. A child who, notes Rancière, has

> a capacity already possessed, a capacity that every person has demonstrated by succeeding, without a teacher, at the most

difficult of apprenticeships: the apprenticeship of that foreign language that is, for every child arriving in the world, called his or her mother tongue. (Rancière 2002)

From an educational point of view, how difficult it is *not* to notice this figure of a child. It is difficult not to give priority to the fact that the presumption of equality is built around a child's capacity to learn language. It is not the case, as various commentators on Rancière would have it, that Rancière has chosen to make equality, pure and simple, his starting point.[5] Rather, he has chosen to make as his starting point a figure that is, for all intents and purposes, off limits to those who deal in the currency of political philosophy. Or rather, the figure of the child is not so much off limits as it is imperceptible. The child has a certain context within the way the sensible is distributed. To speak about equality within the sensible is one thing. Equality is linked, as Kristin Ross puts it, to 'powerful ideologies' (Rancière 1991a, p. xxiii). To speak about a child, within the sensible, is another. It is rather a matter that only a mother or father should appreciate, or only an educational theorist.

Rancière inserts this seemingly educational figure of the child into his discourse on politics. If there are conceptual arguments about politics, about philosophy, about equality and so on, being made in *The Ignorant Schoolmaster*, they are being made with the very real figures of real children. A child does learn a mother tongue. Joseph Jacotot did teach real children. Speaking of this insertion of the real into philosophy, Rancière describes his own efforts to recount the intellectual life of workers in the 1830s:

> Telling the (hi)story of those workers' days and nights forced me to blur the boundary between the field of 'empirical' history and the field of 'pure' philosophy. . . . Philosophy, then, could no longer present itself as a sphere of pure thought separated from the sphere of empirical facts. Nor was it the theoretical interpretation of those facts. There were neither facts nor interpretations. There were two ways of telling stories.
>
> Blurring the border between academic disciplines also meant blurring the hierarchy between the levels of discourse, between the narration of a story and the philosophical or scientific explanation of it or the truth lying behind or beneath it. (Rancière 2007a)

Rancière's use of the figure of the child is of the same practice as this disciplinary blurring. The figure of the child learning his or her mother tongue is one with the rupture of sensibility that describes political engagement. Of course, the fact that it takes an educational theorist to notice this figure of the child who anchors the presumption of equality is not a happy fact. It flatters neither the educational theorist nor the political philosopher. On the one hand, the educational theorist sees too much of the real. On the other, the political philosopher sees too little of it. Both are ensconced in the disciplinary boundaries that Rancière is so often attempting to blur.[6]

Homo Barbarus

We have offered a sketch of the linguistic life of Barbara not because her nascent use of language is in any way unique. And also not because it is in any way representative. In fact, every child steps into the forest of signs in a way that is as random, as interesting, as idiosyncratic, as arbitrary and as wilful, as Barbara's use of these seven words and a grunt. We offered this anecdote first because we feel that it helps to give a fuller picture of just what Rancière is referring to when he notes that

> The human animal learns everything as he has learned his mother tongue, as he has learned to venture through the forest of things and signs that surrounds him, in order to take his place among his fellow humans – by observing, comparing one thing with another thing, one sign with one fact, one sign with another sign. (Rancière 2007a)

Barbara is this human animal learning her mother tongue. She 'ventures into the forest of signs and things that surround' her. So far, she has begun to employ only seven signs, but she has managed to connect these seven signs to no less than thousands of things. She does so 'in order to take her place among her fellow humans', most of whom are family members or close friends, though she will no doubt yell her signs to strangers if they are within earshot. And she widens her understanding of the signs around her, and of the things around her, 'by comparing one thing with another thing, one sign with one fact, one sign with another sign'. A cow, for example, is a 'lola,' but a squirrel is not a 'mulner'. 'Dada' is to be used in her father's absence, but 'mama' is to be used both in her mother's presence and in her absence.

About learning and the figure of the child, Rancière also states that learning one's mother tongue is of a particular quality. Such learning is difficult, as difficult as any learning will ever be. Though first language acquisition is generally relegated to the pre-educational life of the child, Rancière turns this figure of the child-as-emerging-person (or, as we have discussed earlier, child-as-soon-to-be-autonomous-person) on its head. The child with language is not beginning her journey into the world of signs. She has rather been there for a long time, already practising 'the most difficult of apprenticeships'. It is not an easy task for Barbara to figure out exactly what a 'lola' is. One hears the word so often, in so many different contexts. 'Lola' may have, among its meanings, 'The family dog will appear soon', but then again it may not. After all, Lola does not always obey. Lola does not always appear when her name is called. This claim that the mother tongue is 'most difficult' certainly rests upon the irascibility of language. Language is not one with science. It is not one with literature. It is not one with history, geography or any other curriculum that has been penned by human hand. Living, spoken language escapes the codification of educational representation. Especially in the form of one's mother tongue, it can only – *only* – be learned in the random and idiosyncratic ways that children do learn language. It is the most difficult of apprenticeships precisely because one *must* go about learning it on one's own, without the help of a map or a guidebook, without even a teacher who has a plan.

At this point, it might be tempting to say that Rancière's figure of the child is really just an educational figure. One might say that Rancière, by excavating the work of Joseph Jacotot, has presented us with one more in a long line of figures of the child. One might say that Rancière, like Rousseau in his *Emile*, is establishing an educational figure of the child that will then go hand-in-hand with a psychological understanding of the child's intellectual development. This is of course a common practice in educational philosophy, and such figures provide wonderful conceits of the human person for psychologists to work with in order to 'improve' education. It might be said, in this vein, that Rancière is making a psychological claim about human learning, a claim that, in turn, grounds his more important political presupposition of equality. This might be true if Rancière's account of language were less nuanced than it is.[7] It might be true if he were not in a position to assert, as he does:

> We can see that it is a question of philosophy and humanity, not of recipes for children's pedagogy. Universal teaching is above all the universal verification of the similarity of what all the emancipated can do, all those who have decided to think of themselves as people just like everyone else. (Rancière 1991a, p. 41)

THE POLITICS OF LEARNING ONE'S MOTHER TONGUE

That the 'most difficult' apprenticeship of all happens to be learning one's mother tongue, that is, learning a language, is not at all a psychological observation. For this most difficult childhood adventure into language is no different from another most difficult and contentious linguistic practice. It is one and the same as the political adventure into language. Thus, while Rancière's figure of the child might seem at first glance to repeat the time-honoured tradition in educational thought of offering a figure of the child who is to be brought, by means of education and by means of psychological advances in education, *into* the realm of the political; instead, this child is already political even as she is acquiring her first language. That is, she is political even before she goes to school to become autonomous and emancipated. To see how this is so, let us return to the figure of Barbara. We have introduced this child under the name of Barbara, and this name happens to be hers in reality. The name 'Barbara' of course derives from *foreign* or *strange*. It is etymologically linked to the term 'barbarian', the name for those who seem to say only 'bar-bar-bar' because their words are foreign and not understood. In many ways, Barbara lives up to her name at this particular point in her life. Her grunts are no more than 'bar-bar-bar' to most people's ears. Indeed, three of the seven words she uses make no sense to people who do not know her well. So far, three of the seven words she knows of her mother tongue are not precisely of her mother tongue since they have the untranslatable particularity that all proper names have.

The figure of the child inserting herself into language – the figure of the child who speaks – is in fact no different than the figure of the person who engages in what Rancière calls politics. We are not trying to make a comparison here. We are asserting an equivalence. Barbara, as her name happens to suggest, is for all intents and purposes primarily a 'noise' maker at the age of seventeen months. Her babbling,

for the most part, does not contain articulate words within the distribution of the sensible, just as the barbarian's sounds are not articulate
words within the philosopher's city. Indeed, adults use the onomato-
poeic word 'babble' to describe how children speak precisely because
it indicates something foreign sounding like 'bar-bar-bar'. Children
babble in a way that is inarticulate to the existing distribution of the
sensible. In her babbling state, little Barbara is not unlike the plebs in
Rancière's account of Menenius Agrippa: 'There is no place for discussion with the plebs for the simple reason that plebs do not speak.
They do not speak because they are beings without a name, deprived
of logos – meaning, of symbolic enrollment in the city' (Rancière
1999, p. 23). Of course, the child is given a name precisely on the
promise that he or she *will* speak, or at least will have the chance to
speak, sometime in the future. There is not a strict equivalence
between the pleb and the child because the child has a chance to
become a political actor in a way that is foreclosed to the pleb.

At a certain point, then, the child says a word. But, the child does
not say this word as some passive echo of that which she has heard
before. Barbara uses a word with intention. She yells 'nana' in order
to be fed when she is hungry. But at first, her father does not know
what 'nana' means. He does not even know that Barbara can speak.
She will cry when the word 'nana' does not get her what she wants.
She will continue to cry until her father understands what 'nana'
means. 'Politics', writes Rancière,

> exists because those who have no right to be counted as speaking
> beings make themselves of some account, setting up a community
> by the fact of placing in common a wrong that is nothing more
> than this very confrontation, the contradiction of two worlds in
> a single world: the world where they are and the world where
> they are not, the world where there is something 'between' them
> and those who do not acknowledge them as speaking beings.
> (Rancière 1999, p. 27)

A bottle indeed means the world to Barbara at this hungry moment.
A bottle is the world between her and her father. To get to that
bottle, Barbara must not only say something that stands as a sign
for the bottle. She must also gain the right to be counted as a speaker
who can say what she needs to say within the community of speaking
beings.

Once again, this account of a child learning language is not a psychological account. It is rather a political account of stepping into language with all the force that is entailed in any political encounter of the emancipatory sort. Learning one's own language is not 'the most difficult apprenticeship' simply because it entails great intellectual patience. It is not difficult simply because it proceeds by fits and starts, and because it requires copious amounts of verifying and comparing. Nor only because it requires deciphering and re-deciphering signs and their relations to things, signs and their relations to other signs, things and their relations to other things. Learning one's own language is also 'most difficult' because it entails the added intersubjective effort to insert oneself into a distribution of the sensible where previously speech had not existed. This is the intersubjective effort, or force, of a political subject rather than the psychological effort of an atomistic learner. The child does not enter language in an easy, or in a humble, way. The child must force his or her will onto another in order to be understood in a way that reconfigures the distribution of the sensible. 'The repetition of egalitarian words', writes Rancière in *On the Shores of Politics*, 'is a repetition of that forced-entry, which is why the space of shared meaning it opens up is not a space of consensus. . . . To postulate a world of shared meaning is always transgressive. It assumes a symbolic violence both in respect of the other and in respect of oneself' (Rancière 1995a, p. 49).

Underscoring the link between the assumption of political equality and the assumption of equality based upon the child's acquisition of the mother tongue, Rancière, in a 2004 interview, notes the following:

> Jacotot says that, in reality, in order for a master to explain something to a student, the student must already understand the words of the master. There is already an equality in the possession of one's mother tongue, an equality that passes through forms of instruction that are not scholarly forms. (2004b)

What is striking here is the way Rancière makes an obvious parallel between the assumption of equality in the mother tongue spoken by the child, on the one hand, and on the other, the political assumption of equality in his political work that does not focus on children. In his political writings, Rancière repeatedly notes that the equality to be assumed between the oppressed person and the oppressor stems from the fundamental fact that the oppressed can understand the words of the oppressor. For example, in *Disagreement* he writes,

> There is order in society because some people command and others obey, but in order to obey an order at least two things are required: you must understand the order and you must understand that you must obey it. And to do that, you must already be the equal of the person who is ordering you. (Rancière 1999, p. 16)

And while this adult figure of the *equal* unequal figures prominently in Rancière's formulation of political equality, the childhood figure of the student who knows the mother tongue must be understood as a prior example of this same equality. The child who understands the master is a figure of the would-be political actor. Such an actor is assumed to be equal with others as is the child. In each case, one can proceed on the basis of equality because an (assumed) inferior is always already able to understand an (assumed) superior.

We have chosen to examine a particularly contentious entry into language with our sketch of Barbara. A demand of hunger, where her cries led the way, establishing the introduction of a new word, one that was not clearly intelligible to either party before this forced-entry. It would be fair to argue that this sort of forced-entry is an aberration, that it is an exception rather than the rule of the way children insert themselves into language. An exception for two reasons: first because it is unusually violent, and secondly because more often than not children and adults establish communication with words that already exist, signifiers that connote previously acknowledged signifieds. This is a fair argument as far as it goes. 'Calm' uses of 'real' words are certainly more the norm when a child is learning a language (which, by the way, remains intellectually difficult nevertheless). They are much more likely to occur than instances like Barbara's insertion of 'nana' into English. However, this argument, far from proving that the child is not a political exemplar, more properly affords space for a more nuanced linguistic look at Rancière's notion of politics. And once again, we will be able to underscore the fact that the figure of the child in Rancière is political, not psychological.

Let us bracket just for a moment the argument against particularity, against the 'non-calm' and 'non-real' moments of language acquisition, in order to highlight the performative nature of Barbara's use of the word 'nana'. By performative in this case, we are referring to the work of Jacques Derrida, Judith Butler and many others who have used J. L. Austin's example of the declaratory statement, 'I christen thee Titanic', as an example of the sort of auto-creative linguistic moment that is *central* rather than peripheral to linguistic interaction. In this performative sense, Barbara and her father have just created a new name for 'bottle' just as the Titanic becomes the Titanic *as* it is christened. We take Rancière to be working within this tradition of performative analysis. (Incidentally, to return to our sketch of Barbara, when Barbara points to a *different* dog and yells 'lola,' the response by an adult, 'Yes, that is another lola-dog' – this response is an example of performative *re*-iteration. It is an attempt to re-establish Lola's name as *only* Lola's name.) This performative understanding is implied throughout Rancière's work on both politics and poetics. He puts it this way, 'The forms of social interlocution that have any impact are at once arguments in a situation and metaphors of this situation' (Rancière 1999, p. 56). In the simple case of 'nana' coming to mean 'bottle', there was a message being sent by the father that he would indeed accept 'nana' on Barbara's terms, and *in* her terms. The child is, in this case, in the political position 'where it is necessary to produce both the argument and the situation in which it is to be understood' (Rancière 1999, p. 57).

This performative understanding of the speech situation actually serves as a hinge between linguistic experiences that seem 'forced' and those that seem more 'kind'. It also serves as a hinge between linguistic experiences that seem 'non-real' and those that seem 'real'. First on the matter of being forced: When a child establishes a way of speaking for the first time, it matters not whether such a way of speaking *seems* forced or kind. There is, nevertheless, a *symbolic* force that draws a binding acknowledgment, a new metaphor, of the child as speaker, where there was no such metaphor before. The child, who has not spoken before, becomes a speaker for the first time at the same that she speaks for the first time. And at this time, her interlocutor is forced into a position to acknowledge that the child is indeed a speaker. The child speaks, and metaphorically, the child attains the status of speaker from the perspective of the adult world. In *Disagreement*, Rancière calls this the 'understanding of understanding' (Rancière 1999, pp. 44–49). Understanding happens not only at the level of propositional content, but also at the level of ontological status. When a speaker inserts him or herself from the position of noisemaker into a newly configured distribution of the sensible, one first of all calls upon others to understand the words one uses. But secondly, one demands of the other an understanding that one is no longer simply a noisemaker. There is thus an understanding of one's newly acquired status as speaker at the same time that there is an understanding of the words that are spoken. Thus whether it be in the adult world or in the world of the child, a question like 'Do you understand?'

> is an expression that tells us that 'to understand' means two different, if not contrary, things: to understand a problem and to understand an order. In the logic of pragmatism, the speaker is obliged for the success of their own performance, to submit it to conditions of validity that come from mutual understanding. (Rancière 1999, p. 45)

In such cases, the distinction between the force of tears, or the force of smiles, is a psychological distinction quite distinct from, and having nothing to do with, the linguistic force of the child-as-speaker, or the force of understanding's understanding. Once again, Rancière's figure of the child is not psychological, but political. This political status of the child does not depend upon any prior psychological state.[8]

Furthermore, as long as one is in the political position of producing 'both the argument and the situation in which it is to be understood', the distinction between the 'made-up' word and the 'real' word is equally as irrelevant. In a very real sense, *every* word is made up when it is inserted into the order of discourse. Whether Barbara inserts a word like 'nana' into the English language, or whether she inserts a word like 'mama' which already *seems* to be in the language, is quite irrelevant. In both cases, there is a performative enactment that creates an understanding – and an understanding of understanding – that is particular to the specific circumstance where Barbara uses whatever word she uses. While it might seem that 'nana' is somehow more performatively magical than 'mama', the metaphorical force of each word is just as magical in each case. A child has become a speaker. That is what is understood of understanding. Whatever particular word has been used to attain this status is only part of what is at stake in this political enactment.

PAULO FREIRE'S PEDAGOGY OF THE OPPRESSED

We have looked to the figure of the child as a significant link to an understanding of Rancière's work in political theory. Using the figure of the child, it is possible to understand a politics that starts early in life, long before the child is educated, long before the 'stultifying' apprenticeship that generally introduces the child into the realm of the 'sensible' and thus into the realm of the sort of 'policing' that passes for politics. As we have seen, the child in Rancière is political because he or she is a child who inserts him or herself into language. Such insertion is forceful, difficult and full of performative ambivalence. It is ambivalent insofar as it establishes a metaphorics of speakability at the same time that it communicates basic needs, desires and intentions. Importantly, this figure of the child is political rather than psychological. This is important because Rancière's child is not simply another conceit fabricated in order to streamline how we bring children from a position of voicelessness to a position of voice. The psychological figure of the child always assumes a developmental *telos* and this is exactly the sort of *telos* that Rancière is at pains to eschew.

Given Rancière's figure of the child, it is useful to revisit other pedagogies that claim to emancipate the student. The question must be asked: What kind of child do they posit? When one pays attention to the figure of the child, that is to say, to the figure of the student, it is a bit easier to discern whether a particular emancipatory pedagogy is emancipatory through and through. Indeed, the figure of the child in Rancière sets a very high bar. It causes one to wonder just what sort of human being is being assumed by pedagogies that would otherwise claim to emancipate the human being. Unfortunately, with regard to the practice of pedagogies that claims to emancipate the human being, it seems very easy to become so fixated on the injust- ices of society, and the injustices of schooling, that one forgets the very assumptions that are being made about those who are being emancipated through education. One forgets the dubious assumptions that we have noted earlier: that one must be *led* to emancipation, that the one who emancipates knows more than the one who is emancipated, and that the experiences of the one who is emancipated are not to be trusted. By saying this, we do not presume to be saying exactly as Rancière has already said. We are rather presuming to offer another 'intervention' on his work.

Describing his own method in the third person, Rancière writes:

> Let us sum it up: the works of Rancière are not 'theories of', they are 'interventions on'. They are polemical interventions. This does not only mean that they take a political stance. This means that they imply a polemical view of what ideas are and do. (Rancière 2009a, p. 116)

One can also take the figure of the child as such an intervention, in this case an intervention on the idea called 'emancipatory pedagogy'. The figure of the child in Rancière is in fact powerful enough to highlight a particular contradiction within emancipatory pedagogy, a contradiction that might not be highlighted otherwise. The emancipatory pedagogy we have in mind is Paulo Freire's.[9]

THE BANKING MODEL VERSUS PROBLEM POSING

In order to get at the figure of the child presumed by Freire, an overview of his pedagogy of the oppressed is helpful. Then, Freire's work can be set in the context of Rancière's educational thought. At the risk of repeating what is common knowledge, a restatement of Freire's conception of the oppressive 'banking' method – and its emancipatory counterpart, 'problem-posing' education – is a useful way to begin. This method yields at least five oppressive pedagogical operations. First, banking authority is used to dominate the student by separating pedagogy into two parts. Splitting curriculum in an artificial manner; the preparation of content is done by the teacher only. The student is hidden from that preparation, and thus the banker keeps the student out of the loop of human agency. Writes Freire,

> The banking concept (with its tendency to dichotomize everything) distinguishes two stages in the action of the educator. During the first, he cognizes a cognizable object while he prepares his lessons in his study or his laboratory; during the second, he expounds to his students about that object. The students are not called upon to know, but to memorize the contents narrated by the teacher. (Freire 1970, p. 61)

What the banking teacher does in his or her preparation of knowledge ensures that the student's relation to curriculum will not be an agentive one that *engages* with knowledge, but will rather be a passive one that *looks at* pre-digested knowledge. Students are force- fed a rhetoric of conclusions.

Second, banking pedagogy sets up house inside of the student's consciousness, instilling its own slogans and its own policies *within* the student's worldview. Drawing on Hegel's Master/Slave dialectic, Freire describes this situation as the same as the consciousness of the slave who internalizes his or her master's values. Banking educators fill the oppressed 'with slogans which create even more fear of freedom' (Freire 1970, p. 176). The oppressed, ' "housing" the oppressors within themselves . . . cannot be truly human' (Freire 1970, p. 176). This is because the oppressed are 'beings for another' (Freire 1970, p. 31). 'What characterizes the oppressed is their subordination to the consciousness of the master', and this subordination is augmented by the practice of banking authority, a practice that is quite happy to let students experience the world vicariously, as an inauthentic part of the student's self (Freire 1970, p. 31). After being banked, students can no longer think for themselves because their thinking is only borrowed from the teacher. Likewise, they can no longer *be* for themselves because their very being is borrowed from that same teacher. Banking pedagogy uses various psychological means to oppress the student. The banking system employs authority at the expense of the student's freedom. Such authority produces passive students, denies epistemological/existential agency, severs the student from knowledge production, fosters dominant ideologies and introjects itself into student consciousness.

Third, banking authority uses methods that force students into the passive position of an active/passive dichotomy. Some examples of this active/passive dichotomy are 'the teacher teaches and the students are taught', 'the teacher knows everything and the students know nothing', 'the teacher thinks and the students are thought about' and 'the teacher disciplines and the students are disciplined' (Freire 1970, p. 54). In this binary of what-the-teacher-does and what-the-student-does, the teacher is always the initiator of pedagogical practice and the student is always the one for whom such practice is initiated. The banking instructor is an authority figure who takes the active position of oppressor. The student is in the passive position of the one who is oppressed.

Fourth, banking authority uses *epistemological* force to strip the student of human agency. Describing the banking system, Freire shows the convergence of epistemological and existential agency. To know for oneself is also to *be* for oneself. And conversely, to have another person think in one's stead is to lack the ontological position of being completely human. When banking authority is used on a person, such a 'person is not a conscious being (*corpo consciente*); he or she is rather the possessor of *a* consciousness: an empty "mind" passively open to the reception of deposits of reality from the world outside' (Freire 1970, p. 56). Fullness and emptiness are first of all descriptions of *knowledge* that has been acquired or not. At the same time, though, they are descriptions of the extent to which human *existence* is fully, or only partially, actualized. Banking authority forces epistemological passivity onto students, which is in fact no different from forcing them into existential passivity.

Finally, banking authority works as an ideological apparatus. Freire notes that '[banking] education (for obvious reasons) attempts, by mythicizing reality, to conceal certain facts which explain the way human beings exist in the world' (Freire 1970, p. 64). Such a concealing education promotes common sense understandings of the world that are not to be questioned. These are the 'myths' to which Freire is referring. In a banking system, people do not 'develop their power to perceive critically *the way they exist* in the world *with which* and *in which* they find themselves' (Freire 1970, p. 64). Instead, they see their world 'as a static reality' (Freire 1970, p. 64). So, banking authority creates static myths about the world. And, it also creates static myths about language. The very words that come to be used by teachers and students are shrouded in the common sense of dominant ideology. Within the banking system, students are not able to interrogate language. They cannot say 'a true word' (Freire 1970, p. 68).

In contrast to the banking method, Freire encourages a 'problem-posing' method of education. Through problem posing, the five operations of the banking method will be overturned. Students will no longer be thought of as passive and teachers will not act as if they are the only agents in the educational encounter. For example, teachers will be students at the same time that they are teachers and students will be teachers at the same time that they are students (Freire 1970, p. 61). And no longer will the epistemological advantages of the teacher be used to strip agency from the student. Instead, the knowledge of the teacher and the knowledge of the student will be considered to be of equal value. The knowledge of the student will be legitimized, and made equal to the teacher's knowledge, through academic exploration of the student's world. Problem posing education will also solve the problem of the teacher's hidden preparations, and the effect that those preparations have on the student's ability to understand knowledge as something available to all people at all times. This is because problem posing, as an exercise in dialogue, establishes a situation where thinking and knowledge are transparent to, rather than hidden from, the student.

Moreover, problem-posing education will break away from the ideological saturation that typifies instruction. In problem-posing education, the aim of pedagogy will no longer be to pass on the symbols of cultural capital, for these symbols only serve to continue the domination of the oppressed by the oppressors. Instead, problem-posing pedagogy will focus its questions directly *at* the ideological 'truths' that oppressors use to enact their own agenda. The ideological reality of the oppressed, rather than that of the oppressor, will be the focus of inquiry of the problem-posing method. And finally, the problem-posing method will never ask students to take on the values of their teachers, the values of oppressors. Because problem-posing begins with the student's reality rather than with the teacher's reality, the student will never be asked to substitute an alternative consciousness for his or her own.

RANCIÈRE AND FREIRE

Rancière's work and Freire's appear at first glance to have some things in common. Indeed, it might seem that Freire's depiction of the banking method is a true gloss on Rancière's account of the stultifying pedagogue. For example, when Freire offers his brilliant account of the banking instructor who diligently prepares materials before class, in the 'laboratory', and then proceeds to deliver instruction as if such intellectual effort was never necessary, it is possible to accept this as a concrete example of stultification in Rancière's sense. To be sure, Rancière's account of stultification in *The Ignorant Schoolmaster* echoes this sort of epistemological mystification felt on the part of the student: 'The student feels that, on his own, he wouldn't have followed the route he has just been led down; and he forgets that there are a thousand paths in intellectual space open to his will' (Rancière 1991a, p. 59).

Freire's account of the banking instructor in his laboratory is convincing and it seems to bolster Rancière's story of the knowing – as opposed to the ignorant – schoolmaster. The oppressor, or the knowing master, hides his intellectual labour with the express purpose of astounding the student. This astounding is calculated. The teacher-as-oppressor prepares enough beforehand in order to guarantee that every student will be sure that he or she could not have arrived at knowledge without the master.

It might also seem that Freire's appeal to the Hegelian logic of alienated consciousness gives another gloss on the feeling of stultification as presented in Rancière's *Ignorant Schoolmaster*. Describing the stultification of even the Socratic method, Rancière (using the words of Jacotot) notes:

He [the Socratic teacher] orders turns, marches, and counter-marches . . . From detour to detour, the student's mind arrives at a finish that couldn't even be glimpsed at the starting line. He is surprised to touch it, he turns around, he sees his guide, the surprise turns into admiration, and that admiration stultifies him. (Rancière 1991a, p. 59)

Freire appeals to a psychic dynamic of oppression which parallels this observation of Jacotot's. Thus, it might be surmised that Freire has sketched a parallel account of oppressed student consciousness, one that jibes with, and in fact augments, the image of the stultified student, one that includes a vivid description of the passive student's 'empty mind' (Freire 1970, p. 56). It is indeed the case that students and teachers often employ this metaphor of emptiness. The trope of knowledge as a positivity, and mind as a bucket waiting to be filled, is rife in education and elsewhere. This trope no doubt helps to augment the image of infinite regress established by the social logic of pedagogical progress that Jacotot and Rancière have described. As the student learns that there is no end to his or her quest for knowledge, that there will always be another instructor with another path to some further truth, it does make sense that a certain negative self-image accompanies this infinite quest. The mind, as Freire points out, is usefully, and oppressively, understood as a container for collecting various bits of knowledge all along the way. And with this metaphor of emptiness goes its opposite. The knowing schoolmaster, for his part, is already full. He or she stands as a source of constant comparison as one who has already arrived.

THE FIGURE OF THE CHILD IN PAULO FREIRE: THE CHILD DOES NOT SPEAK

Yet whatever similarities might exist between Friere's banking method, on the one hand, and the stultifying techniques of the knowing master, on the other, we want to ask a different question: What is the figure of the child in Freire's emancipatory pedagogy? Ultimately, Freire's figure – as we will note again with regard to the politics of recognition, and with regard to the student as speaker – is psychological, not political. It should be clear to anyone who reads this summary of banking education and its antidote the problem-posing method, or to anyone who studies the work of Freire, that the application of the problem-posing method is a means by which to bring students from one psychological state to another. It is through the problem-posing method that an imbalanced psychic equation of teacher-over-student will change into a state of psychic balance between teacher and student. Whether the student stands astounded at the intellectual prowess of the teacher, or whether the student learns that she herself is the one who is astounding; whether the student is a being-for-the-other, or a being-for-self; whether the student sees herself as an empty vessel waiting passively to be filled, or whether the student comes to the more proper realization that she is always already full herself; in short, Freire's figure of the child remains a psychological one (see Bingham 2002, 2008, pp. 129ff.).

There is nothing wrong with this psychological figure of the child aside from the fact that such a child *does not speak*.[10] Or rather, this child does not speak in the political sense that we have been describing, in the sense that one must speak if one is to insert oneself from noise into language. The psychological figure of the child in Freire is a form. It presents a set of either/or's: Either the child is astounded or the child is astounding. Either the child is a being-for-the-other or the child is a being-for-self. Either the child is empty of the positivity of knowledge or the child is full. In these alternatives of either/or, it may indeed be the case that one side of the binary is a more agentive state, and that one is less agentive. Indeed, as far as Freire's account takes us, it is of course more desirable to be astounding, for-oneself, and full. But such a psychological form leads one *either* to one side or to the other, either to oppression or to freedom. In this scenario, the role of education is faced with one of two circumstances: Either the child is free or the child is oppressed. If the child is free, then there remains no role for the pedagogy of the oppressed – and thus emancipatory pedagogy stands as tautology. If the child is oppressed, then the emancipatory teacher is to work with the child, using a particular method, so that the child might become free from domination. One sets to work on creating the conditions for those who are not free to become free.[11]

Why does this child not speak? The psychological child does not speak because it has already been decided *for* the child how and when he or she will speak. It has been decided by the selection of a particular method that will bring him or her to speech. In Freire's case, it is the problem-posing method. The child, under a psychological description, cannot proceed in an arbitrary manner, and certainly not 'from proximity to proximity' (Rancière, this volume, p. 4).[12] Rather, he or she is part of a project that gives order to social arbitrariness. Psychology explains. It explains because it is part of the explanatory order. It explains how human beings, and in this particular case, how the child, is an ordered form, a form that can and must be brought to speech in an orderly way.

But language has an arbitrariness that will not be ordered. In *On the Shores of Politics*, Rancière writes:

> Jacotot alerted the egalitarians to the impossibility of binding two contradictory logics: the egalitarian logic implied by the act of speaking and the inegalitarian logic inherent in the social bond. There could never be any coincidence between the two different senses in which the speaking being is prey to arbitrariness: to the arbitrariness of language on the one hand and to the arbitrariness of the social bond on the other. (Rancière 1995a, p. 81)

When one inserts oneself into language from noise, there is an arbitrariness that cannot be anticipated beforehand. This arbitrariness cannot be prepared for. Yet, the psychological figure of the child presumes that there is preparatory work to be done before certain children can speak. Specifically, there must be an explanation of the child before he or she can be prepared to speak. Then, this explanation must be used to teach the child in a certain way. Only after the child is taught in a certain way will he or she be able to speak. Under the psychological figure of the child, then, one forgets that a child such as Barbara has already spoken. Rancière reminds us that children already speak. They already speak politics.

The psychological figure of the child – the figure of the child that needs psychological description in order to speak – has a long history, a history that Freire joins. Rancière uses Plato's *Republic* to illustrate the yearning for psychological and social order that is characteristic of the sciences of the individual and collective soul.

> This republic is not so much based on law as universal as on the education that constantly translates the law into its spirit. Plato invents . . . the sciences that go with this internalization of the bond of community, those sciences of the individual and collective soul that modernity will call psychology and sociology. (Rancière 1999, p. 68)

It is of course useless to try to claim that we live in educational circumstances that exist as a direct result of Plato's proclamations, or that Freire's work is somehow conscientiously Platonic. Rather, it is important to acknowledge the similarities that do exist between education's consistent re-application of psychology and sociology, and the order and harmony that the 'sciences of the individual and collective soul' are said to offer a society. In education, psychology and sociology are incessantly proffered as a way to, first, describe the figure of the child and, then, to recommend educational remedies based on such a psychological or sociological figure. Freire's work is no exception to this sort of application of psychology. Freire offers a figure of the child who suffers under psychological oppression, then he offers a method of pedagogy to relieve this suffering. Freire's work ultimately serves to bring harmony into the individual soul of the oppressed.

In Freire's work, the psychological oppression of the student is answered by the liberating practice of the problem-posing educator. This is exactly the point where Rancière's figure of the child is completely at odds with Freire's. For Rancière, the task is not to restore psychological order to the stultified child. Instead, the task it to assume that the child is already equal to another. It is to assume that the child has already been political. It is to assume that the child has already undergone the most difficult of apprenticeships. This assumption of equality is precisely why a psychological orientation cannot have a place in the emancipatory master's practice. With a psychological orientation, one must take the child as one who progresses, one who moves towards emancipation, as one who benefits from a pedagogical method in order to attain the 'maturity' that Kant advocates. For Freire, then, it is only natural that there is a pedagogy of the oppressed – that there is a particular method – by which the oppressed can arrive at emancipation. For Rancière, there can be no such method because the child is already assumed to be an equal being, a being who is already political, a being whose only method is established only by being un-established. The child's method is an arbitrary method. It is the arbitrary method of language that will not follow a social or psychological logic. It is a method saying, doing and feeling. The child does not need, in fact cannot possibly use, the master's method in order to become emancipated. The child already speaks. That is the child's method. The child needs no knowledge from the master to speak again.

In sum, we find it notable that Jacques Rancière has joined a long line of educational thinkers in offering a figure of the child. Notable, not because he follows in the venerable tradition of positing a figure for others to use as a conceit for streamlining and improving education, but because he offers a figure that resists such easy conceits. Rancière's figure of the child resides in the arbitrary forest of signs. This childhood figure initiates a presumption of equality that is central to Rancière's work. Unfortunately, it is likely that this figure will be subsumed under more weighty conceptual matter, that is, under the psychology and sociology of equality, unless those concerned with equality begin to understand the social world more as Rancière does, in all its linguistic arbitrariness, and without distinction between the 'childish' talk of education and the more 'serious' talk of politics.

CHAPTER 4

INCLUSION IN QUESTION

The guarantee of democracy is not the filling up of all the dead times and empty spaces by the forms of participation or of counterpower: it is the continual renewal of the actors and of the forms of their actions, the ever-open possibility of the fresh emergence of this fleeting subject.

(Rancière 1995a, p. 61)

INTRODUCTION

The central position of the idea of 'equality' in Rancière's writing might suggest that his work would sit comfortably within a tradition of political thinking and political action that aims to make the democratic polity more inclusive – with the ultimate aim of making democracy *all*-inclusive. After all, Rancière's suggestion to start from the assumption of equality seems to suggest a political order in which all have an equal part. In this chapter, we review Rancière's ideas in relation to discussions about democracy and inclusion. We do this in order to highlight a distinction between two 'trajectories' of democratization, one that has inclusion as its *telos* and one that has equality as its starting point. Whereas the first, in a sense, knows where it wants to go, the second only knows where it wants to start. As a result of this difference, the idea of 'inclusion' operates in a fundamentally different manner, which not only has implications for what we might call the practice of democratic politics but also has implications for what we might refer to as the style of political theory. In this chapter, we take up themes and ideas introduced in the previous chapters in order to show how these might intervene in discussions about inclusion and democracy. Education, as we will see, cannot be left out of this discussion because just as it is considered to be a central force in the process of emancipation, a particular educational logic is also inscribed in ways of thinking about inclusion and democracy.

DEMOCRACY AND INCLUSION

The idea of inclusion plays a central role in discussions about democracy. It could well be argued that inclusion is one of the core values, if not *the* core value of democracy (see, for example, Allan 2003; Gundara 2000; Young 2000). The 'point' of democracy, after all, is the inclusion of the demos – which ultimately means the whole *demos* – into the ruling (*kratein*) of society. This is why Pericles defined democracy as the situation in which 'power is in the hands not of a minority but of the whole people' (Held 1987, p. 16) and it is why Aristotle wrote about democracy as the 'rule of all over each and of each by turns over all' (ibid., p. 19). It is also reflected in Abraham Lincoln's definition of democracy as 'the government of the people, by the people, and for the people' (Torres 1998, p. 159) and in David Beetham's and Kevin Boyle's more precise definition of democracy as entailing 'the twin principles of popular control over collective decision-making and equality of rights in the exercise of that control' (Beetham and Boyle 1995, p. 1). All this, however, is not only a question of definition but also affects the legitimacy of democracy. As Iris Marion Young has pointed out, the normative legitimacy of democratic decision-making precisely depends 'on the degree to which those affected by it have been included in the decision-making processes and have had the opportunity to influence the outcomes' (Young 2000, pp. 5–6).

Inclusion is not only the main point and purpose of democracy, it is also one of its main problems. The question that has haunted democracy from day one (and in a sense already troubled democracy before it took off) is the question 'Who are the people?' – or, to put it differently: 'Who are to be included in the (definition of the) *demos*'? This is the question of *democratic citizenship* and it is known all too well that in the city-state of Athens citizenship was a highly restricted affair. Only Athenian men over the age of 20 were eligible for citizenship, while women, children, slaves (who made up about 60% of the population) and immigrants, even from families who had settled in Athens several generations earlier, were simply excluded from political participation (see Held 1987, p. 23). The history of democracy can be written as a continuous quest for inclusion. Some of the most powerful and successful social movements of the last century have precisely mobilized 'around demands for oppressed and marginalized people to be included as full and equal citizens' (Young 2000, p. 6). But, the history of democracy is not only a history of inclusion, it is at the very same time a history of exclusion. In some cases, exclusion has been justified in the very name of democracy. This is, for example, the case with the idea of liberal democracy where the democratic principle of popular rule (expressing the principle of *equality*) is qualified by a set of basic liberties – the freedoms of thought, speech, press, association and religion; the right to hold personal property; the freedom to vote and hold public office; and freedom from arbitrary arrest and seizure as defined by the concept of the rule of law – that takes priority over popular rule in order to make sure that popular rule does not restrain or obstruct individual freedom (thus expressing the principle of *liberty*) (see Gutmann 1993, p. 413; see also Mouffe 2000).

Whereas liberal democracy seeks to exclude certain *outcomes* of democratic decision-making (and thus would exclude those who would argue for such outcomes), there is also a more direct link between democracy and exclusion. The overriding argument here focuses on those who are deemed not to be 'fit' for democracy, either because they lack certain qualities that are considered to be fundamental for democratic participation – such as rationality or reasonableness (see below) – or because they do not subscribe to the ideal of democracy itself. As Bonnie Honig (1993) has argued, this is not only an issue for communitarians who wish to see democratic politics organized around particular political identities. It is also an issue for liberals since they tend to restrict political participation to those who are willing and able to act in a rational way and who are willing to leave their substantive conceptions of the good life behind them in the private sphere. Such strategies not only result in the exclusion of those who are considered to be 'sub-rational' (e.g., certain categories of psychiatric patients) or unreasonable. The strategies are also used to justify the exclusion of those whom we might call 'pre-rational' or, in a more general sense, 'pre-democratic' – and children are the most obvious example of such a category. It is here that there is a strong link with education, as the task of education in democratic societies is often seen as that of making individuals ready for their future participation in democratic deliberation and decision-making – an idea which puts education before and outside of democracy, thus suggesting that politics and education can simply and easily be separated and kept apart (for a critical discussion of this assumption see Biesta 2007; 2010).

While there are, therefore, important questions to be asked about the question of inclusion in democratic theory and democratic practice, this is not to suggest that no attempts have been made to address the question of inclusion. In the next section, we discuss recent developments in political philosophy and democratic theory that are precisely intended to increase the inclusivity of democratic processes and practices. We discuss these developments not only to show that the question of inclusion is of ongoing concern, but also in order to indicate the particular way in which inclusion, democracy and democratization are connected in these discussions. This, in turn, will allow us to show where and how Rancière's thinking about democratization introduces a difference.

VARIETIES OF DEMOCRATIC INCLUSION

In contemporary political theory, two main models of democratic decision-making prevail: the *aggregative* model and the *deliberative* model (see Elster 1998, p. 6; Young 2000, pp. 18–26). The first model sees democracy as a process of aggregating the preferences of individuals, often, but not exclusively, in choosing public officials and policies. Two central assumptions of this approach are that the preferences of individuals are taken as given, and that politics is primarily concerned with the aggregation of preferences, often, but not exclusively, on the basis of majority rule. Where these preferences come from, whether they are valid and worthwhile or not, and whether they are held for egoistic or altruistic reasons, are seen as irrelevant questions. The *aggregative* model assumes, in other words, 'that ends and values are subjective, non-rational, and exogenous to the political process' and that democratic politics is basically 'a competition between private interests and preferences' (Young 2000, p. 22).

Over the past decades, an increasing number of political theorists have argued that democracy should not be confined to the simple aggregation of preferences – democracy as counting and adding up – but should involve the *deliberative transformation* of preferences. Under the deliberative model, democratic decision-making is seen as a process which involves 'decision making by means of arguments offered *by* and *to* participants' (Elster 1998, p. 8). Crucially, this includes decision-making both about the means and about the ends of collective action. As Young explains, deliberative democracy is not about 'determining what preferences have greatest numerical support, but [about] determining which proposals the collective agrees are supported by the best reasons' (Young 2000, p. 23). The reference to 'best reasons' indicates that deliberative democracy is based upon

76

a particular conception of deliberation. John Dryzek, for example, points out that deliberation can cover a rather broad spectrum of activities but argues that for *authentic* deliberation to happen the requirement is that the reflection on preferences should take place in a *non-coercive* manner (see Dryzek 2000, p. 2). This requirement, so he explains, 'rules out domination via the exercise of power, manipulation, indoctrination, propaganda, deception, expression of mere self-interest, threats . . . and attempts to impose ideological conformity' (ibid.). This argument resonates with Jon Elster's claim that deliberative democracy is about the give and take of arguments by participants 'who are committed to the values of rationality and impartiality' (Elster 1998, p. 8), and with his suggestion that deliberation must take place between 'free, equal and rational agents' (ibid., p. 5).

In one respect, the 'deliberative turn' is an important step forward in democratic theory and democratic practice. The deliberative approach seems to be a more full expression of the basic values of democracy, particularly the idea that democracy is about actual participation in collective decision-making. In the aggregative model, there is, after all, little participation, and decision-making is almost algorithmic. Moreover, the deliberative approach seems to have a much stronger educational potential. In the deliberative model, 'political actors not only express preferences and interest, but they engage with one another about how to balance these under circumstances of inclusive equality' (Young, 2000 p. 26). Young argues that because this interaction 'requires participants to be open and attentive to one another, to justify their claims and proposals in terms of [being] acceptable to all, the orientation of participants moves from self-regard to an orientation to what is publicly assertable' (ibid.). Thus, 'people often gain new information, learn different experiences of their collective problems, or find that their own initial opinions are founded on prejudice and ignorance, or that they have misunderstood the relation of their own interests to others' (ibid.). Or, as Warren has put it, participation in deliberation can make individuals 'more public-spirited, more tolerant, more knowledgeable, more attentive to the interests of others, and more probing of their own interests' (Warren 1992, p. 8). Deliberative democracy, so its proponents argue, is therefore not only more *democratic* but also more *educative*. A third asset of deliberative democracy lies in its potential impact on the *motivation* of political actors in that participation in democratic decision-making is more likely to commit participants to its outcomes. This suggests that deliberative democracy is not only an intrinsically desirable way, but probably also an effective way, of social problem solving (see Dryzek 2000, p. 172).

The deliberative turn can be seen as an attempt to bring democracy closer to its core values and in this respect represents an important correction to the individualism and 'disconnected pluralism' (Biesta 2006, p. 89) of the aggregative model and of liberal democracy more generally. However, by raising the stakes of democracy, deliberative democracy has also brought the difficulty of democratic inclusion into much sharper focus, and thus has generated – ironically but not surprisingly – a series of problems around the question of inclusion. The main issue, so we wish to suggest, lies with the *entry conditions for participation* in deliberation. Writ large, the discourse on deliberative democracy tends to suggest that participation in democratic deliberation should be regulated and that it should be confined to those who commit themselves to a particular set of values and behaviours. Young, for example, argues that the deliberative model 'entails several normative ideas for the relationships and dispositions of deliberating parties, among them inclusion, equality, reasonableness, and publicity' which she claims 'are all logically related in the deliberative model' (Young 2000, p. 23). Proponents of deliberative democracy specify a set of entry conditions for participation, although what is interesting about the discussion is that most go at great pains to delineate a *minimum* set of conditions necessary for democratic deliberation rather than an ideal set (see, for example, the contributions in Elster 1998).

Young provides an interesting example of this with her distinction between *reasonableness* (which she sees as a necessary entry condition) and *rationality* (which she does not see as a necessary entry condition). For Young being reasonable does not entail being rational because of the fact that reasonableness refers to 'a set of dispositions that discussion participants have [rather] than to the substance of people's contributions to debate' (Young 2000, p. 24). She concedes that reasonable people 'often have crazy ideas', yet 'what makes them reasonable is their willingness to listen to others who want to explain to them why their ideas are incorrect or inappropriate' (ibid.). In Young's hands reasonableness thus emerges as a communicative *virtue*, that is, as a criterion for judging the quality of how people interact, and not as a criterion for the logical quality of people's preferences and convictions. This not only shows why the issue of inclusion is so prominent in the deliberative model. It also explains why the deliberative turn has generated a whole new set of issues around inclusion. The reason for this is that deliberation is not simply a form of political decision-making but first and foremost a form of political *communication*. The inclusion question in deliberative democracy is therefore not so much a question about who should be included, who should be 'counted in' – although this question should be asked always as well. It is first and foremost a question about who is able to participate effectively in deliberation.

As Dryzek aptly comments, the suspicion about deliberative democracy is 'that its focus on a particular kind of reasonable political interaction is not in fact neutral, but systematically excludes a variety of voices from effective participation in democratic politics' (Dryzek 2000, p. 58). In this regard, Young makes a helpful distinction between two forms of exclusion: *external exclusion*, which is about 'how people are [actually] kept outside the process of discussion and decision-making', and *internal exclusion* where people are formally included in decision-making processes but where they may find, for example, 'that their claims are not taken seriously and may believe that they are not treated with equal respect' (Young 2000, p. 55). Internal exclusion, in other words, refers to those situations in which people 'lack effective opportunity to influence the thinking of others even when they have access to forms and procedures of decision-making' (ibid.). Such internal exclusion can in fact be the unintended outcome resulting from the emphasis of some proponents of deliberative democracy on 'dispassionate, unsituated, neutral reason' (ibid., p. 63).

To counteract the internal exclusion that is the product of a too narrow focus on argument, Young has suggested several other modes of political communication which should be added to the deliberative process not only to remedy 'exclusionary tendencies in deliberative practices' but also to promote 'respect and trust' and to make possible 'understanding across structural and cultural difference' (ibid., p. 57). The first of these is *greeting* or *public acknowledgement*. This is about 'communicative political gestures through which those who have conflicts . . . *recognize* others as included in the discussion, especially those with whom they differ in opinion, interest, or social location' (ibid., p. 61; emphasis in original). Young emphasizes that greeting should be thought of as a starting-point for political interaction. It *'precedes* the giving and evaluating of reasons' (ibid., p. 79) and does so through the recognition of the other parties in the deliberation.

The second mode of political communication is *rhetoric* and more specifically the affirmative use of rhetoric (ibid., p. 63). Although one could say that rhetoric only concerns the form of political communication and not its content, the point Young makes is that inclusive political communication should pay attention to and be inclusive about the different forms of expression and should not try to purify rational argument from rhetoric. Rhetoric is not only important because it can help to get particular issues on the agenda for deliberation (see ibid., pp. 66–67). Rhetoric can also help to articulate claims and arguments '*in ways appropriate to a particular public in a particular situation*' (ibid., p. 67; emphasis in original). Rhetoric always accompanies an argument by situating it 'for a particular audience and giving it embodied style and tone' (ibid., p. 79). Young's third mode of political communication is *narrative* or *storytelling*. The main function of narrative in democratic communication lies in its potential 'to foster understanding among members of a polity with very different experience or assumptions about what is important' (ibid., p. 71). Young emphasizes the role of narrative in the teaching and learning dimension of political communication. 'Inclusive democratic communication', so she argues, 'assumes that all participants have something to teach the public about the society in which they dwell together' and also assumes 'that all participants are ignorant of some aspects of the social or natural world, and that everyone comes to a political conflict with some biases, prejudices, blind spots, or stereotypes' (ibid., p. 77).

It is important to emphasize that greeting, rhetoric and narrative are not meant to *replace* argumentation. Young stresses again and again that deliberative democracy entails 'that participants require reasons of one another and critically evaluate them' (ibid., p. 79). Other proponents of the deliberative model take a much more narrow approach and see deliberation exclusively as a form of *rational* argumentation (see, for example, Benhabib 1996) where the only legitimate force should be the 'forceless force of the better argument' (see Habermas 1988, p. 47). Similarly, Dryzek, after a discussion of Young's earlier work, concludes that 'argument always has to be central to deliberative democracy' (Dryzek 2000, p. 71). Although he acknowledges that other modes of communication can be present and that there are good reasons to welcome them, their status is different 'because they do not have to be present' (ibid.). For Dryzek, at the end of the day all modes of political communication must live up to the standards of rationality. This does not mean that they must be subordinated to rational argument 'but their deployment only makes sense in a context where argument about what is to be done remains central' (ibid., p. 168). Whereas all this may well be true, we shouldn't forget where the importance of Young's contribution exactly lies, because what she tries to do is address the particular forms of exclusion generated by deliberative democracy, that is, those forms of internal exclusion that result from the fact that deliberative democracy specifies a particular form of political *communication*. To put it bluntly, internal exclusion is simply not an issue for the aggregative model because there it is only the counting that counts.

INCLUSION, POLICE AND POLITICS

The foregoing discussion clearly reveals the central role of the idea of inclusion in recent discussions in political philosophy and democratic theory. Both deliberative democracy and Young's amendments aim to make the democratic process more inclusive by proposing a different 'agenda' for democracy – one which suggests a shift from aggregation to deliberation – and by creating opportunities for more to take part and hence for fewer to be excluded from the democratic process. We might refer to this strategy as a *quantitative* conception of inclusion since the ultimate aim is to add individuals to the democratic order. Inclusion appears in this discussion as a process in which those who stand outside of the sphere of democracy are brought into this sphere and, more importantly, are brought into this sphere by those who are already on the 'inside', so to speak. The assumption here is that inclusion is a process which happens 'from the inside out', a process which emanates from the position of those who are already considered to be democratic. The very language of inclusion not only suggests that someone is including someone else. It also suggests that someone is setting the terms for inclusion and that it is for those who wish to be included to meet those terms. This is clearly visible in the way in which proponents of deliberative democracy stipulate minimal entry conditions for participation in democratic deliberation. Deliberative democracy asks people to be reasonable and to commit themselves to the force of the better argument. Anyone who is willing to do so, and who is able to do so, is more then welcome, and education is often positioned as the central 'enabler' in relation to this, that is, as the institution that is supposed to make children and other newcomers 'ready' for democracy.

This also reveals a second assumption underlying the discussion, which is the belief that democracy can become and should become a normal situation. In the discussion about inclusion, the main challenge seems to be perceived as a *practical* one; that is, as the question how we can make our democratic practices even more inclusive (through, for example, Young's notion of 'internal inclusion') and how we can include even more people into the sphere of democratic deliberation (through Young's notion of 'external inclusion'). The assumption here is that if we can become even more attentive to otherness and difference, we will eventually reach a situation of total democratic inclusion, a situation in which democracy has become normal. While people may have different views about *when* this situation might be reached (in the nearby future or in a very distant, utopian future), *how* it might be reached (by converting more and more people to the 'gospel' of democracy or by continuously adjusting and fine-tuning democratic practices and principles) and whether or not there will always be some remainders (see Mouffe 1993), the idea that democratization means including more and more people into the sphere of democracy reveals the underlying idea that the best democracy is the most inclusive democracy, and reveals the underlying assumption that democracy can and should become a normal political reality.

Stated in this way, and using Rancière's vocabulary, we can begin to see that the trajectory of democratization specified in recent discussions on democracy and inclusion is actually about the construction of a particular police order and of the insertion of those outside of this order into the order. The trajectory of democratization thus appears as a *teleological* trajectory in that the ideal 'end state' is already known and defined, so that inclusion becomes entirely a numerical operation. Even if an 'advance' like deliberative democracy adds some qualitative nuance to what sort of person is allowed to be included, and what sort is to be excluded – nevertheless, it is still a matter of 'counting' some in and some out. In the end, it's still a matter of quantity. Moreover, it becomes a controlled operation because of the fact that those on the 'inside' of the particular order claim the right to police the borders of the order and set the entry conditions for inclusion. One of the implications of Rancière's distinction between the police order and the process of politics is, as we have discussed earlier, that the police order is not necessarily bad. In this regard, it might indeed be the case that steps should be taken to make the existing police order more inclusive seriously. But what

Rancière's distinction does allow us to do in addition to this – and here his ideas introduce a fundamentally different way to approach questions of inclusion and democratization – is to indicate the *limitations* of a strictly quantitative view of inclusion.

The main limitation of a quantitative view is that inclusion can only be conceived in terms of the adoption of *existing* identities or subject positions. One might consider the following thought experiment: Suppose a group of children decide that they want the right to vote. Since it is only the adult who presently is allowed to vote, the logic of inclusion into a set of existing identities would indicate that a child must be deemed an adult in order to vote. So let's say a child wants to vote. It is not necessarily the case that she wants to be *an adult* who votes. Not all children want to be adults. Many do not. In such a case, the project of inclusion is left in a quandary since it has already defined the voter as necessarily being an adult – or in what amounts to the same sort of qualification, following Young's thinking on deliberative democracy, as necessarily being *rational*. In such a situation, there is actually no possibility that the 'child' can vote. Such an identity can never exist. Rancière points out another alternative.

> *Man* and *citizen* [and here we might substitute *child* and *voter*] do not designate collections of individuals. Man and citizen are political subjects. Political subjects are not definite collectivities. They are surplus names, names that set out a question or a dispute (*litige*) about who is included in their count. Correspondingly, *freedom* and *equality* are not predicates belonging to definite subjects. Political predicates are open predicates: they open up a dispute about what they exactly entail and whom they concern in which cases. (Rancière 2004c, p. 303)

For a child to vote, it will not suffice to simply add the child's name to the number of those who can vote. The political predicates 'child' and 'voter' must themselves become open to dispute.

The point of politics, after all, is about the *reconfiguration* of the space 'where parties, parts, or lack of parts have been defined' (Rancière 1999, p. 30). Political activity 'makes visible what had no business being seen, and makes heard a discourse where once there was only place for noise' (ibid.). It is

> a mode of expression that undoes the perceptible divisions of the police order by implementing a basically heterogeneous assumption,

Politics – a mode of expression

that of a part of those who have no part, an assumption that, at the end of the day, itself demonstrates the sheer contingency of the order [and] the equality of any speaking being with any other speaking being. (ibid.)

When Rancière argues that democracy is 'not a regime or a social way of life' but should rather be understood 'as the institution of politics itself' (ibid., p. 101), it is precisely in order to highlight the democratic 'deficit' of any police order. This, as we have seen, does not mean that every police order is necessarily bad – there is, after all, 'a worse and a better police' (ibid., pp. 30–31) – but it is to indicate that just adding elements to an existing order does in no way affect the particular distribution of identities and subject positions. It is important not to forget in this regard that not any reconfiguration of the police order would count as politics and hence as an instance of democratization. Rancière clearly restricts this to the encounter of the police process with the process of equality. Democratization appears in this constellation as a practical 'test' of the assumption of equality, that is, of the equality between any and every speaking being (see ibid., p. 30). This is why for Rancière's the 'trajectory' of democratization is anything but teleological. Equality does not appear as a desired end state, but as the starting point that requires constant verification in an open, experimental and non-teleological manner. And, it is for this reason that Rancière's insistence on equality is precisely not a plea for inclusion if, that is, we think of inclusion as the insertion into an existing police order. For Rancière, democratization is therefore not to be understood in numerical terms, but as a qualitative change, as a redistribution and reconfiguration. It is important to see that such a qualitative change not only results in the creation of new identities and subject positions but at the very same time alters the existing identities and subjectivities, at the very least because of the fact that existing identities and subjectivities end up in a different network of relationships. After all, to be a man with voting rights means something different in a police order in which only men have voting rights than in a police order in which men and women have voting rights. This is another reason why for Rancière democratization is not and cannot be understood as a numerical process.

CONCLUSIONS

The aim of this chapter has been to situate Rancière's contribution within contemporary discussions about democracy and inclusion.

Whereas at first sight Rancière's insistence on equality could give the impression that his views are part of a wider ambition to make democracy more inclusive, we have tried to show that because of the fact that for Rancière equality operates as the starting point for politics and not as its *telos*, the trajectory of democratization becomes one that is radically different from where contemporary work in the field of democracy and inclusion is going. In Rancière's work, democracy appears as something that is *sporadic* (see Rancière 1995a, p. 41); it only occurs from time to time and in very particular situations and never denotes a normal situation. Moreover, for Rancière democratization is a process that operates from the outside in, so to speak, rather than from the inside out. Along these lines, Rancière helps to expose the limitations of a numerical conception of democratization that is only after the expansion of the existing democratic order. We wish to emphasize one more time that Rancière's work helps to expose the *limitations* of such a strategy by showing that it operates exclusively within a given distribution of the sensible and does not alter or reconfigure this distribution itself. There may be important gains in taking up existing identities and subject positions – think, for example, of the case of young people 'coming out' with a particular sexual identity. Rancière's work does *not* suggest that such strategic moves are not helpful, or not necessary, rather just the contrary (see Ruitenberg in press). But what distinguishes such processes from those that are about the reconfiguration of the police order, is that only in the latter equality itself is at stake, whereas in the former the existing distribution of the sensible remains unaffected. This is one reason why, with Rancière, we might want to reserve the terms 'democracy' and 'democratisation' for such qualitative changes of the distribution of the sensible rather than for strictly quantitative shifts.

Rancière's intervention in discussions about democracy and inclusion not only hints at different political practices, but also exposes the extent to which political philosophy and democratic theory is implied in the reproduction of the police order. Rancière's extraordinary thinking therefore also has implications for what, in the introduction to this chapter, we have referred to as the 'style' of political theory itself. To this question we now turn.

Recognitive paradigms are policing
* Critique of recognition / intervention on the politics
of recognition

* Polemical staging

* Stultifying movements of
recognitive politics

CHAPTER 5

RECOGNITION'S PEDAGOGY

Police order

Intervention
in the politics ; Their explanatory
of recognition   tendencies

While social struggles are today commonly understood as demands for recognition, we have intimated that for Rancière struggles for recognition miss the mark of the political. This is to say, struggles for social recognition are more properly a matter of the police order than they are a matter of politics. In what follows, we will look more closely at how struggles for recognition are themselves ensconced within paradigms that are policing rather than emancipatory. We will do so in a way that has not, in fact, been articulated by Rancière himself, but in a way that remains germane to Rancière's thought, and especially to the educational significance of his thought. To show how recognitive paradigms are policing, we will use education as a tool. That is to say, we will show that Rancière's educational thinking offers a concrete way to understand that current debates over recognition in political philosophy are actually part of a stultifying pedagogy that is more policing than political. Thus, one aim in this chapter is to offer a critique of recognition or, in Rancière's terms already noted, it is to offer an 'intervention' on the politics of recognition (Rancière 2009a, p. 116). This intervention will be carried out by using emancipatory education as a tool to underscore the stultifying movements of recognitive politics. Another aim of what follows will be to offer a wider critique on the way that scholarship is so often conducted without heed to its own stultifying tendencies. At the same time that we make what Rancière might call a 'polemical' staging of the politics of recognition, we also intend to question the general will to order that characterizes academic research (Rancière 2009a, p. 116). Our intervention on recognition should be construed as an intervention on the explanatory tendencies of so much research that goes on in the humanities and social sciences.

ed Sig
recog ×

intervention

Scholarship

Will to
order

Intervention?
Will to order ; explanatory
tendencies of SS

POLITICAL PHILOSOPHY AND THE RECOGNITION/
REDISTRIBUTION DEBATE

To intervene on the politics of recognition, it is helpful to specify just what is currently at stake in recognitive politics so that the parameters of what we are dealing with are out in the open. To this end, we look to the work of Nancy Fraser and Axel Honneth, both of whom have been advocating a recognitive understanding of politics for some time now. The 'struggle for recognition', as it is currently known in political philosophy, is a description of social struggle that attempts to further the project of Critical Theory by finding a certain 'transcendence' within social 'immanence' (Fraser and Honneth 2003, p. 238). That is, there is an attempt to discern a coalescing of social form (transcendence) and social experience (immanence) that can give rise to emancipatory work. The human need for positive recognition is thus taken as both a psychologically observable fact and a theoretical grid for rectifying injustice. The recognitive tradition in political philosophy derives from Hegel's early Jena writings as well as form the famous Master/Slave dialectic in the *Phenomenology of Spirit* (Hegel 1983, 1977).

These are quick ways to orient oneself to the political theory of recognition. However, even with such brief introductory sentences to recognitive theory, a shock of differences must be noted between recognition's contemporary philosophical advocates.

For her part, Fraser does not rely much on Hegel nor is she impressed with recognition's philosophical genealogy as a way to establish the 'transcendence' of recognition. Instead, she relies on her understanding of current social movements. She invokes what she calls a 'folk paradigm' of recognition: 'Tacitly presupposed by social movements and political actors, folk paradigms are sets of linked assumptions about the causes of and remedies for injustice' (Fraser and Honneth 2003, p. 11). For Fraser, the folk paradigm of recognition and the folk paradigm of redistribution are the two main logics informing present day struggles in civil society. Thus, recognition and redistribution

have both a philosophical and a political reference. Philosophically, they refer to normative paradigms developed by political theorists and moral philosophers. Politically, they refer to families of claims raised by political actors and social movements in the public sphere. (Fraser and Honneth 2003, p. 9)

In this way, Fraser's analytic of recognition is less concerned with the 'transcendence' of Critical Theory and more with its 'immanence'.[1] Yet, it is this focus on immanence that gives Fraser some sharp analytic tools that enable her readers to appreciate the subtle grada- tions of recognition. For example, she is able to describe specific instances of identity recognition, or identity misrecognition, at the same time demonstrating that the struggle for recognition can never be disentangled from the struggle for the distribution of goods. In this sense, Fraser's proximity to immanence yields lived specificities that the phenomenological tradition of Hegel glosses over.

To offer one example of Fraser's focus on the particular, and to show how Fraser's analytic skills are served by specific cases, it is helpful (and 'educational') to attend her recognitive reasoning on the French ban on headscarves:

> Consider the French controversy over the *foulard*... some French republicans have argued that the *foulard* is itself a marker of [female] subordination and must therefore be denied recognition. Disputing this interpretation, however, some multiculturalists have rejoined that the scarf's meaning is highly contested in French Muslim communities today, as are gender relations more generally; thus instead of construing it as univocally patriarchal, which effectively accords to male supremacists the sole authority to interpret Islam, the state should treat the *foulard* as a symbol of Muslim identity in transition, one whose meaning is contested, as is French identity itself.... In my view, the multiculturalists have the stronger argument here. (Fraser 2003, pp. 41–42)

There are a few things to note about Fraser's recognitive account here. First of all, she advocates a pragmatic approach to recognition based on participatory parity rather than self-actualization. This means that Fraser's account of the struggle for recognition never asserts that positive recognition should be an end in itself simply because such positive recognition will enhance human flourishing. Fraser's participatory parity approach means that she will *not* advocate that the *foulard* be worn in order to enhance the self-worth of students. On the contrary, Fraser takes the *foulard* as a cue for deliberation on matters of differing attributions of cultural status: 'Differences in its interpretation notwithstanding, the norm for participatory parity serves to evaluate such recognition claims deontologically, without any need for ethical evaluation of the cultural or religious practices in question' (Fraser 2003, p. 42).

Second, the *foulard* stands as a reminder that for Fraser recognitive struggles most properly take place on what she calls the 'cultural or symbolic' level. As Fraser puts it,

> The remedy for cultural injustice . . . is some sort of cultural or symbolic change. This could involve upwardly revaluing disrespected identities and the cultural products of maligned groups. It could also involve recognizing and positively valorizing cultural diversity. More radically still, it could involve the wholesale transformation of societal patterns of representation, interpretation, and communication in ways that would change *everybody's* sense of self. Although these remedies differ importantly from one another, I shall henceforth refer to the whole group of them by the generic term 'recognition'. (Fraser 1997, p. 15)

That recognition is symbolic and cultural is central for Fraser's 'perspectival dualism' (Fraser and Honneth 2003, p. 64). In this way, she can keep redistribution, which is material, distinct from recognition, which is symbolic. This is not to say that struggles for recognition do not entail material aspects, nor that struggles for redistribution do not entail symbolic aspects. Fraser's close attention to particular, lived struggles teases out the imbrication of the symbolic and the material with both recognition *and* redistribution. As she notes, 'Even the most material economic institutions have a constitutive, irreducible cultural dimension. . . . Conversely, even the most discursive cultural practices have a constitutive, irreducible political-economic dimension' (Fraser 1997, p. 15). Nevertheless, recognition for Fraser is, in its purest form and for the purposes of her political analysis, a matter of culture and symbol.

One more aspect that figures centrally in this account of the *foulard* is Fraser's willingness to understand culture as mutable, and thus recognition as potentially transformative. She contrasts transformative recognition with affirmative recognition, linking the former to deconstruction and the latter to mainstream multiculturalism according to the following grid:

	Affirmation	**Transformation**
Redistribution	*the liberal welfare state* surface reallocations of existing goods to existing groups, supports group differentiation; can generate misrecognition	*socialism* deep restructuring of relations of production; blurs group differentiation can help remedy some forms of misrecognition
Recognition	*mainstream multiculturalism* surface reallocations of respect to existing identities of existing groups; supports group differentiations	*deconstruction* deep restructuring of relations of recognition; destabilizes group differentiation (Fraser 1997, p. 27)

As should be evident from this grid, Fraser's acuity at using specific lived experiences to illustrate nuance where there is a struggle for recognition, this acuity is matched by her keen ability to map academic theorizing onto those very same struggles. In this case, her own folk paradigms of mainstream multiculturalism and deconstruction serve as dialectic exemplars in much the same way that symbol and materiality do elsewhere.

Of course, the struggle for recognition is itself a struggle. If Fraser can claim that no one position of symbol or materiality maps precisely onto the struggle for recognition, it can be similarly claimed that the struggle for recognition itself entails what Rancière calls 'social arbitrariness' (Fraser 1995, p. 71). The struggle for recognition itself is a contested paradigm that only a fiction of social continuity can hold together. Citing the firm ground of philosophical, historical and psychological tradition that Fraser notes only in passing, Axel Honneth claims to grasp, in a way more profound than Fraser, both the transcendence and the immanence of recognition. He claims a transcendence more secure than Fraser.

[Fraser's] error here lies in the tacit premise that 'social movements' can serve critical social theory as a kind of empirically visible guiding thread for diagnosing normatively relevant problem areas. What such a procedure completely overlooks is the fact that official designation as a 'social movement' is itself the result of an under-ground struggle for recognition. (Fraser and Honneth 2003, p. 120)

Thus, Honneth identifies the struggle for recognition as a foundation for all political action. He assails the nuance of Fraser's analysis as 'one-sided' and as 'an over-generalisation of American experience' (Fraser and Honneth 2003, p. 118). For Honneth, all needed nuance derives from the philosophical nuance of Hegel, the historical nuance of Marxist class struggle and the psychological nuance of D. W. Winnicott and George Herbert Mead. In short, Honneth assails Fraser's specific cases (such as the *foulard* controversy in France, which, by the way, is not exactly a generalization of American experience) as following, coming after, the venerable paradigm of recognitive struggle, rather than setting its terms.

Honneth's account of recognition shows how social suffering can serve as a ground for ethical, social and political theory. He begins from the perspective of self-realization, considering recognition to be 'the satisfaction of a generic human need'.[2] This human need for recognition finds voice at three levels of social interaction:

> In terms of the new kind of individual self-relation made possible by the revolution in the recognition order, this means that subjects in bourgeois-capitalist society learned – gradually, and with many class- and gender-specific delays – to refer to themselves in three different attitudes: in intimate relationships . . . in legal relations . . . and, finally, in loose-knit social relations – in which, dominated by a one-sided interpretation of the achievement principle, there is competition for professional status – they in principle learn to understand themselves as subjects possessing abilities and talents that are valuable for society. (Fraser and Honneth 2003, p. 142)

Honneth thus posits recognition as a beginning and an end point. Social suffering begins at the level of love, law or political action. And, social suffering can be addressed at these three levels through various measures that restore feelings of positive recognition.

In contrast to Fraser's dialectic of symbol and materiality, Honneth treats misrecognition as a source of feeling. It is social suffering itself, rather than the form of misrepresentation that may

Honneth

Feeling

have caused the suffering, that propels individuals to struggle for dignity at home, for rights in the legal system and for status in society at large. So, recognition is a matter of feeling. Furthermore, since recognitive struggle in any one of these spheres may entail material remedies, Honneth need not distinguish so starkly between redistribution and recognition, not even for heuristic purposes. Instead, since recognition is both the beginning and end point of a continuum from social suffering to self-realization, redistribution is instrumental to recognition rather than at odds with it. Interestingly, though, there is a significant linguistic component to Honneth's project. For, Honneth is concerned that social suffering has been too often experienced without being articulated. While social suffering has long been the cause, and the telos, of social movements, Honneth sees himself

Moral grammar

Semantic Bridge

as the spokesperson for, indeed as the teacher of, a 'moral grammar' that will allow individuals to articulate the connection between feelings of misrecognition, on the one hand, and social action, on the other. Honneth's work is thus supposed to construct a 'semantic bridge' between feeling and action. His work is to construct a lexicon for the everyday feelings of misrecognition that have been identified in theory by Hegel, Mead and others. While Fraser construes recognition as a matter of representation and interpretation, Honneth construes it as a matter *in need of* representation and interpretation.

Because Honneth's account of recognition is largely psychological and only narrowly discursive, it is difficult to discern whether the symbolic realm is figured as a mutable form, and thus whether recognition can lead to discursive transformation. Fraser is certainly critical of Honneth on this point, and accuses him of 'recognition monism' as a result of the uniformity she senses in his understanding of social suffering (Fraser and Honneth 2003, p. 215).

> [Honneth's] appeal to a stratum of experience that is simultaneously empirical and primordial is incoherent. An instance of 'the myth of the given', it fails to appreciate that we can never have access to moral experience unmediated by normative discourses, as the latter necessarily infiltrate not only the experiences of social actors but also the perspectives of those who study them. (Fraser and Honneth 2003, pp. 204–205)

It does seem that Honneth's insistence on a recognitive grounding for all social action leaves little room for a transformation of seeing, saying and doing. Because any such transformation is, following Honneth, restricted from reconfiguring his transcendent psychological account of personal injury; and, because his psychological account of personal injury overdetermines the presumed cause of all social action; as a result, most of what is seen, said, and done in the realm of the symbolic/cultural realm is already affixed to a presumed transcendence of the interpersonal psychology of recognition. In short, the *reasons* for social action cannot be contested. They are already determined by Honneth, Hegel, Mead and others.

RANCIÈRE'S POLITICS AND RECOGNITION'S POLICE

It is tempting to use the work of Rancière to discount *all* political philosophy with broad strokes, and thus to discount the efforts of Fraser and Honneth *tout court*. It is tempting to recall this statement by Rancière: 'what is called "political philosophy" might well be the set of reflective operations whereby philosophy tries to rid itself of politics, to suppress a scandal in thinking proper to the exercise of politics' (Rancière 1999, p. xii). Along these lines, one might summarily discount the very tradition of political philosophy, and thus discount scholarly arguments such as Fraser's and Honneth's, as part and parcel of this tradition that attempts to kill politics as Rancière defines it. 'I am not', notes Rancière,

> a political philosopher. My interest in political philosophy is not an interest in questions of foundations of politics. Investigating political philosophy, for me, was investigating precisely into what political philosophy looked at and pointed at as the problem or the obstacle for policy and for a political philosophy, because I got the idea that what each found in their way of foundation might well be politics itself, might be something else or something more that disrupts the right order of policy. (Rancière 2003b)

Politics – as distinct from political philosophy – as we have seen disturbs the police order. It speaks *differently* by reconfiguring the distribution of the sensible. The work of Fraser and Honneth, it might be said, gives order rather than rendering voice to disorder. It does the work of policing rather than the work of politics. Such work follows the tradition inaugurated by Plato when he introduced those ordering discourses of psychology and sociology into his republic. In Rancière's words that we have seen before:

> This republic is not so much based on law as a universal as on the education that constantly translates the law into its spirit. Plato . . . invents the sciences that go with this internalisation of the bond of community, those sciences of the individual and collective soul that modernity will call psychology and sociology. (Rancière 1999, p. 68)

Indeed, such a wholesale discounting seems all the more plausible when we recall that the avowed aim of recognitive theorists is to work within, indeed between, the parameters established by Plato on the one hand and by Aristotle on the other. The Platonic project, as described by Fraser, 'adopts the mindset of latter-day philosopher kings', where 'the answers to our questions will resemble blueprints, whether in the utopian guise of overarching institutional designs or in the realist guise of policy proposals for piecemeal reforms' (Fraser and Honneth 2003, p. 70). An Aristotelean approach, in contrast, assumes 'the standpoint of democratic justice, seeking to foster citizen deliberation about how best to implement the requirements of justice' (Fraser and Honneth, 2003, p. 70). Fraser places herself squarely between Plato and Aristotle, trying to avoid the pitfalls of each. As she states of her own work, it aims 'to avoid both the Scylla of monologism and the Charybdis of proceduralism' (Fraser and Honneth 2003, p. 72) by discerning 'the point at which theoretical argumentation rightly ends and dialogical judgment should begin' (Fraser and Honneth 2003, p. 71).

One might indeed use Rancière's thinking to discount this between-Plato-and-Aristotle approach, especially after considering Rancière's account of philosophy's deep-seeded 'hatred of democracy'. Rancière shows that both Plato and Aristotle were in fact concerned with calming the radicality, the ruling by lots, of authentic democracy.[3] He calls these two regimes of anti-political calming by the names of 'archipolitics' and 'parapolitics'. 'Archipolitics, whose model is supplied by Plato, reveals in all its radicality the project of a community founded on the integral realisation, the integral sensibility of the *arkhê* of the community, ceaselessly replacing the democratic configuration of politics', Rancière writes in *Disagreement* (Rancière 1999, p. 65). Plato's is a political philosophy based on the organization of society according to the various abilities of those governed. There is one particular thing that each person can do best, and such a one thing will be each person's lot. The interests of those governed are not considered, but their abilities are. In this scheme, political philosophers also do one thing best. They come up with ideas on what others need to do best. Parapolitics, on the other hand, acknowledges the centrality of those who are governed, even if such centrality is acknowledged only because it serves a ruler. 'The Aristotelian solution, as we know, is to turn the [parapolitical] problem around. . . . The sole means of preserving tyranny will thus be for the tyrant to submit to the rule of law and to promote the material betterment of the people' (Rancière 1999, p. 73). Both archipolitics and parapolitics offer programs to avoid the scandal of authentic democracy, the former through seamless integration of each from each, the latter through the material betterment of those who might otherwise seek to overthrow the tyrant. Given such a less-than-flattering genealogy of archipolitics and parapolitics, it is certainly tempting to dismiss a program of political philosophy that actually boasts this very lineage.

In this vein, it is indeed possible to look at the content of Honneth's objections to Fraser, as well as the content of Fraser's objections to Honneth, as just another example of the way that political philosophy continues to work between the poles of archipolitics and parapolitics at the expense of the very authentic democracy one might otherwise assume them to be working towards. As previously noted, both Honneth and Fraser use the tradition of Critical Theory to accuse one another of not living up to critical standards of engaging the subtle interplay between transcendence and immanence. In fact, the space of Critical Theory, thus described, concerns nothing other than the theoretical instantiation of the space between archipolitics and parapolitics, nothing other than the space between 'architheory' and 'paratheory'. Architheory is that which properly supplies a blueprint for politics to proceed. From the theorist comes what the theorist knows best, namely, theory. Paratheory, for its part, accepts the tyrant's realization that theory itself stands to be unravelled by those whom theory concerns. Since Critical Theory concerns those who are wronged, it must listen to those who are wronged so as not to be undone by the specificity of their concerns. His position being closer than Fraser's to architheory, Honneth accuses Fraser of paying too much attention to specific, North American cases of misrecognition without 'doing justice to what 'transcendence' could mean' (Fraser and Honneth 2003, p. 238). Honneth accuses Fraser of not being architheoretical enough. She listens too much to those who are wronged. She is undone not by those who are wronged, but by a lack of theoretical mediation. Fraser, for her part, holding a position closer to paratheory than architheory, accuses Honneth of the opposite. By not listening closely to those who are wronged, Honneth falls prey to 'the Scylla of monologism' (Fraser and Honneth 2003, p. 72).

While it is possible and perhaps reasonable to proceed in this fashion, by highlighting the limitations of the debate over recognition as a subset of the all debates in political theory that have been framed by a discernable 'hatred of democracy', it is also possible to proceed in a different fashion, in a way that utilizes Rancière's educational thinking rather than his political thinking. Above, we thematized a few tenets of Rancière's work on politics – his dismissal of political philosophy *per se*, his distinction between politics and policing, his conventions of archipolitics and parapolitics. We suggested that it is tempting to analyze the recognitive debate along the lines of these tenets. It is certainly the case that recognition is part of a philosophical discourse on politics that is easy to critique from Rancière's political perspective. For, Rancière has set a standard for critique of political philosophy by demonstrating that political philosophy is, in its genealogy as well as its practice, a matter of policing rather than a matter of what he terms 'politics'. But there is, lingering in adult debates about what is political and what is not political about recognition, about who is truly a Critical Theorist and who is not, about where one situates oneself on a spectrum between archipolitics and parapolitics – there is a child lingering, a student who goes to school. What we will outline here is the pedagogical apparatus that is concomitant with Rancière's work in political philosophy. This pedagogical apparatus offers a way to understand the political discourse on recognition in a different light, in a way that might be overlooked if one is content to remain within the central tenets of Rancière's own work on politics. This is not to discount the above comments on the incommensurability between political philosophy in general, recognitive debate in particular, and 'politics' as it is outlined by Rancière, but to follow Rancière's own border-crossing form of theorizing onto the terrain of education.

THE PEDAGOGY OF POLITICAL PHILOSOPHY

By way of following the debate over recognition onto the terrain of education, it is instructive to look at the way Rancière characterizes Plato's inauguration of political philosophy not only as an 'archipolitics', but also as a *pedagogy* of archipolitics. 'It is important to see', writes Rancière, 'how the idea of a republic, the project of education, and the invention of the sciences of the individual and collective soul hold together as features of the archipolitical apparatus' (Rancière 1999, p. 69). The project of education is itself entwined with the project of archipolitics, and with the project of parapolitics. And Rancière reminds us that this pedagogical project is not simply a way of understanding things past.

> The Republic of Jules Ferry, a paradise supposedly lost of the universalism of the citizen, was born in the shadows of the liberal and social sciences, which were themselves a legacy of the archipolitical project. The school system and the republic have not just recently been perverted by psychology and sociology. They have merely changed brands of psychology and sociology, and changed the ways teachings about the individual and collective soul work within the system of knowledge distribution, redistributed the relationship of pedagogical mastery, the anarchy of the democratic circulation of knowledge and the republican development of harmony between personality and morality. (Rancière 1999, p. 69)

This passage warrants some comment. Rancière is here describing the supposed fall from grace of modern educational institutions. Recent conservative critiques of the French educational system have accused psychology and sociology – in other words, they have accused progressive education as a paradigm for the continuous improvement of education on personal and social levels – of derailing a more venerable tradition of education. In the words of Rancière, 'the power of equality resided, for republican ideology, in the universality of knowledge equally distributed to all, without consideration of social origin, in a school well-removed from society' (Rancière, this volume, p. 11).

But on the contrary, this supposed venerable tradition of education should be more properly understood as being already ensconced in a set of political assumptions premised on a particular way of 'hating democracy'. Education, even in its 'republican' form, is still an instantiation of the originary elements of political philosophy, in particular, the two elements that were always psychological and sociological, tending to the development of the soul and the social body. Education, in 'republican' as well as progressive forms, is an effort to quell 'the anarchy of the democratic circulation of knowledge' (Rancière 1999, p. 69). Like political philosophy that still unabashedly sifts between the poles of archipolitics and parapolitics, education entails a concerted effort to put each person in a particular place according to his or her particular ability all the while claiming to 'promote the material betterment of the people' (Rancière 1999, p. 73).

For the purposes of moving from Rancière's educational analysis into the political philosophy of recognition, it is also instructive to remember the particular lesson that he draws from Jacotot. For Rancière, Jacotot represents not only a way of construing education, but also a way of construing the social order at a particular moment in history.

> The years of the jacotist polemic indeed correspond to the moment when a reconstituted social order is being put into place after the upheaval of the French Revolution. It is a moment when one wants to achieve revolution, in all senses of the word 'achieve', to pass from the age of critique with its destruction of monarchical and divine transcendencies to the 'organic' age of a society based on its own, immanent reason. (Rancière, this volume, p. 7)

The school was to be the tool for this achievement of immanence. Yet, Jacotot stands as a reminder of someone who saw the folly of this supposed role of the school. Or more specifically, he saw the folly of explanatory pedagogy, which is another way to say the folly of the school, in achieving such immanence. He saw the explicative order as just another way to 'hate democracy' as democracy has always been hated. The lesson that Rancière draws from this particular juncture in history is that 'people's education is not simply an instrument, a practical means of working to reinforce the social order. It is actually an 'explanation' of society; it is a working allegory of the way that inequality is reproduced by 'making visible' equality' (Rancière, this volume).

Thus, the lesson Rancière draws from Jacotot is much different from the lesson that Bourdieu, Passeron and other 'reproduction theorists' draw from the form of the school. It is not simply that the school functions to *reflect* or *reproduce* the social order, and more specifically, the political philosophy of Western democracies. Rather, the school *explains* society by demonstrating, through explanation, that everything that needs to happen in society can be rectified, changed or improved by means of explanation. In this way, the practice of explanation, a practice that is lodged primarily at school but that is itself replicated throughout society, is more than itself. It is also a 'working allegory' for how society must function. This working allegory does indeed reflect and reproduce the social order, but that is not all that it does. It also reproduces a certain explicative understanding of social order. It reproduces a certain complacency with explanation, a complacency that ignores the inequality that explanation itself always brings forth. It is the basis of a 'humanity pedagogicized' (Rancière 1991, p. 120). From Jacotot we learn:

> Every social order, relying on explication, thus includes all other explications and especially rejects the method of intellectual emancipation, based as it in on the futility and even the danger of explication in teaching. (Rancière 1991, p. 105)

For the purposes of teasing out the implications of this working allegory, this 'explanation of society' as a society that explains, we will take Rancière at his word. What might this allegory of explanation explain? How might this allegory of explanation explain what it explains?

Indeed, that one can ask such questions of education, and of the explicative regime it inaugurates, is one of Rancière's unique contributions to educational thought. It is unique precisely because this contribution inverts the common ways that one usually thinks about education. First and foremost, education is usually considered to be a practice that is informed by other disciplines, or other bodies of knowledge, rather than being a practice that informs other disciplines, other bodies of knowledge. Or, as is the case in reproduction theory, education is considered a practice that reproduces societal norms and hegemonic ways of thinking. Or, as in the case of critical theories of resistance, education is seen as a venue for resisting societal norms and hegemonic ways of thinking. This contribution

educational logic

of Rancière's, this practice of using an educational logic to cast light on matters that most often refuse identification with education, is a practice not only to be observed, but also to be employed. To this end of taking Rancière at his word, one can ask the following questions *about* political philosophy from the perspective of education. Doing so means doing otherwise than assuming that education must remain the child, *answering* all the questions that other strands of thought put to him or her. Rather, it is possible for education to ask the questions. For example, in the present case, does the allegory of educational explanation explain the debate over recognition in political philosophy? How might it do this explaining? These are educational questions about recognition. They derive from the heart of that which education reflects, reproduces and, of course, explains – explanation itself.

THE TEACHINGS OF NANCY FRASER AND AXEL HONNETH

Rancière's insistence on the form of the school in political philosophy reminds us that debates about the body politic constitute a teaching as well as a theory. It is easy to overlook this fact. It is easy to disregard the fact that a debate in political philosophy not only constitutes an argument, but it also performs *the teaching of an argument*. This is why we maintained earlier that it is 'tempting' to assail political philosophy in a straightforward manner, based on central tenets of Rancière's political thought. It is easier to look at the ostensible logic of an argument than to look, at the same time, at what this argument is performing. The theorizing of recognition is, in its most obvious form, the theorizing of recognition. But at the same time, this theorizing is a teaching. When Nancy Fraser and Axel Honneth write a book entitled *Redistribution or Recognition?* and publish it with Verso Press, they are doing something more than attempting to eke out royalties from the sales of a book. They are doing something more than attempting to augment their academic credentials. They are doing something more than joining in a venerable scholarly debate. While Fraser and Honneth may be doing these things, they are doing something more. They are offering an explanatory teaching to those who are willing to read their book. They are partaking in the form of the school that has, since Plato's archipolitics and Aristotle's parapolitics, offered increasingly refined variations of psychology and sociology to negotiate the poles of transcendence and immanence.

Political philosophy in the form of the debate over recognition is itself a form of pedagogy, a part of 'the project of education and the invention of the sciences of the individual and collective soul' (Rancière 1999, p. 67). It is part of 'the education that constantly translates the law into its spirit' (Rancière 1999, p. 68).

Like all lessons that are taught by persons other than ignorant schoolmasters, the lesson of recognition proceeds in an explanatory fashion. Fraser, for her part, explains the various aspects of cultural recognition and its counterpart, material redistribution. She conducts her explanation with meticulous attention to the grid we saw above. On one axis are the objects of her teaching – redistribution and recognition. On the other axis, the qualities these two attributes can attain – affirmation or transformation. Fraser explains that redistribution and recognition can be thought of as prototypical endpoints on a continuum that, in reality, is a flexible continuum. There is always recognition in redistribution, and there is always redistribution in recognition. Similarly, affirmation and transformation serve as prototypical endpoints, used for heuristic purposes only. There is always transformation in affirmation, and there is always affirmation in transformation. The explanatory nature of Fraser's argument is, indeed, no different than the explanatory nature of all learned schoolmasters when they teach their students.

> Pedagogical logic appears as the act that lifts a veil off the obscurity of things. Its topography is that of top to bottom, of surface to depth. The explicator is the one who carries obscure depth to the clear surface, and who, conversely, brings the false appearance of the surface back to the secret depths of reason. (Rancière, this volume, p. 4)

Fraser sets up her diametric oppositions in such a way that they appear to illuminate four ideal forms: redistribution, recognition, affirmation and transformation. These forms are brought to the clear surface of an analytic grid. Thus, Fraser's teaching is typical of the learned, rather than the ignorant, schoolmaster first because of its ability to bring these ideal forms into the light of day. As she states, 'For practical purposes, then, virtually all real-world axes of subordination can be treated as two-dimensional' (Fraser and Honneth 2003, p. 25).

A second feature follows from her lesson. As she explains her analytic grid, she simultaneously discounts those less-learned people, those students, who may have had prior knowledge of her subject. As noted previously, she explains that her grid is loosely based upon what she calls 'folk paradigms' of redistribution and recognition that are used already, if unwittingly, by people engaged in social struggles. 'Tacitly presupposed by social movements and political actors, folk paradigms are sets of linked assumptions about the causes and remedies for injustices' (Fraser and Honneth 2003, p. 11). However, folk paradigms have 'common associations' that are 'misleading' (Fraser and Honneth 2003, p. 11). Thus, Fraser begins her argument in *Redistribution or Recognition* by saying, 'In what follows, accordingly, I will suspend these common associations' (Fraser and Honneth 2003, pp. 11–12). Fraser's own teaching thus eliminates the muddled thought that precedes it. As all learned schoolmasters, she 'distinguishes between the depths of reason's learned order, and the horizontal ways of the self-taught who move from proximity to proximity, comparing what they don't know to what they do know' (Rancière, this volume, p. 4). Fraser mentions explicitly that which most teachers do not bother to mention. She understands that there are similarities between her learned thought and the thought of the people for whom she presumes to speak, but these similarities are superficial only. While people may know of redistribution and recognition, their knowledge proceeds by 'sets of linked assumptions', 'common associations', 'from proximity to proximity'. People do not, however, know the logic of their knowledge. Such logic must be explained by a master explicator.

Third, there is an assumption about explanation itself that is performed by this teaching. The assumption is that the social order can and should be explained. As we have seen, Fraser puts this assumption as follows: 'For practical purposes, then, virtually all real-world axes of subordination can be treated as two-dimensional' (Fraser and Honneth 2003, p. 25). This is the will to ordered knowledge that Rancière identifies in all political philosophy. It is the tendency to assume that 'social arbitrariness' can be described in a non-arbitrary way, and that such description will be beneficial to others (Rancière 1995a, p. 81). It is the explanatory paradigm set in motion by Plato's archipolitics. To repeat: 'This Republic is not so much based on law as a universal as on the education that constantly translates the law into its spirit' (Rancière 1999, p. 68). Saying that the social order can and should be explained is to say that it can and should be taught, that people who would otherwise use folk paradigms can and should learn to use the paradigms supplied by the teachers of the social order. It is not, after all, necessary to ask what reasons there are for writing a book like *Redistribution or Recognition*. The book explains itself at the same time that it explains the social order, at the same time that it explains that the social order can and should be explained. The debate on recognition proves itself to be a teaching. Like all instruction, 'It is a practical means of working to reinforce the social order. It is actually an "explanation" of society; it is a working allegory' (Rancière, this volume, p. 8).

Honneth's work also proceeds in an explanatory fashion. His avowed aim to establish a 'moral grammar of social conflict,' a 'semantic bridge,' between the personal experience of social suffering on the one hand, and social action on the other, makes sense not only within the rarified context of research in Critical Theory. This grammatical aim is also quintessentially a matter of pedagogy. It is pedagogical in that it seeks to give a new language of recognition to those who presumably do not have fluency in this language to begin with. Honneth puts it this way:

> Hurt feelings of this sort can, however, become the motivational basis for collected resistance only if subjects are able to articulate them within an intersubjective framework of interpretation that they can show to be typical for an entire group. In this sense, the emergence of social movements hinges on the existence of a shared semantics that enables personal experiences of disappointment to be interpreted as something affecting not just the individual himself or herself but also a circle of many other subjects. (Honneth 1996, pp. 163–164)

This theme of a 'shared semantics' is instructive in both senses of the word. It is instructive in the sense that Honneth aims to *teach* political subjects a political Esperanto that will enable them to understand their own feelings of disrespect as feelings that are typical to other members of the entire group of subjects who have such feelings.

It is also instructive in the sense that this particular linguistic trope reveals precisely the difference between one who teaches in the fashion of an ignorant schoolmaster and one who teaches in the fashion of the master explicator. The ignorant schoolmaster, for his or her part, knows that arbitrariness is a quality of all language.

Arbitrariness is that quality which must be grappled with by every child as he or she undergoes 'the most difficult of apprenticeships: the apprenticeship of that foreign language that is, for every child arriving in the world, called his or her mother tongue' (Rancière, this volume). The ignorant schoolmaster knows, 'There could never be any coincidence between the two different senses in which the speaking being is prey to arbitrariness: to the arbitrariness of language on the one hand and to the arbitrariness of the social bond on the other' (Rancière 1995, p. 81). It is the child's successful struggle with the arbitrary nature of the word that gives the ignorant schoolmaster the right to presume that subjects are equal. The learned explicator, on the other hand, does not agree that language is arbitrary. Such an explicator assumes that all language can be codified and taught according the grammar, or the semantics, that an instructor creates in order to facilitate the student's acquisition of language. Such an explicator assumes that the arbitrariness that the child faces in acquiring his or her mother tongue, and the way such a child proceeds in learning this arbitrariness, 'from proximity to proximity', is an aberration (Rancière, this volume, p. 4). The explicator assumes that a grammar must first be established. Only after such a grammar is established, can there be a proper teaching that employs a proper grammar.

It is not simply an extended musing on Honneth's poor choice of metaphor that allows one to say that he is this sort of teacher rather than that sort. It would not matter if Honneth had used a different metaphor. He might have said simply that he wanted to establish 'a bridge' or 'a connection' or 'a way' for political subjects to interpret and to communicate their personal experiences of disappointment. The fact remains that interpreting and communicating are still part of the arbitrariness of language. Whatever *curriculum* is derived from Honneth's efforts to reconstruct the philosophical, psychological and sociological history of the concept of recognition; whatever this curriculum is called, whether or not it is called a language or a grammar, it is still part of an explanatory teaching where the students of such a teaching are those political subjects who need to learn another way of understanding what they have already felt. Honneth's students are those who have feelings of disappointment. From Honneth's point of view, these feelings have been experienced in the same way that a child might experience language for the first time. For Honneth, this is an unfortunate fact. For the master explicator, this is not proper learning. It is childish experience that proceeds 'from proximity to proximity' (Rancière, this volume, p. 4). A political subject should not learn in such a way. A political subject needs a proper curriculum, a proper grammar (Honneth 1996, p. 163).

It should be noted, though, that if Honneth is an explicator, he is at least a progressive explicator. Honneth explains that his project of building a grammar of recognition is established with the explicit aim of letting political subjects speak for themselves of their own social suffering. As he details, he might have chosen to be prescriptive with the recognitive paradigm. He might have insisted that all social affront be transformed into social action by direct appeal to the experience of misrecognition. Instead, he has chosen to supply political agents with a grammar to *discuss* misrecognition. He has given them a grammar to discuss different nuances of their social suffering, including the possibility that their suffering needs a remedy that is more material-based rather than symbol-based. As Honneth puts this,

> It is left entirely open whether social groups employ material, symbolic, or passive force to publically articulate and demand restitution for the disrespect and violation that they experience as being typical. (Honneth 1996, p. 163)

As progressive explicator, Honneth provides the grammar to be learned by his students, but his students, for their part, are free to have conversations among themselves on how to use that grammar. They are encouraged to discuss among themselves in the fashion of the most democratic of classrooms.

By describing the work of Fraser and Honneth in terms of explanatory pedagogy, we are not trying to establish that the political philosophy of recognition is somehow too academic, and thus not connected to the more practical world of 'real' politics. Of course, it does seem, upon reading this work, that it has a certain academic flavour that is ironically at odds with the lives of the very social agents it attempts to explain. When Fraser writes of inaccurate 'folk paradigms' (Fraser and Honneth 2003, p. 11) and when Honneth writes of social agents who selfishly sense only their 'personal experiences of disappointment' (Honneth 1996, p. 163), it is possible to think of this condescension in typical terms of the academic researcher who is out of touch with reality. However, such an account misses the

[margin note: integral Pedagogicisation of society]

point that even the often-used dichotomy – between academics who are out of touch with reality, and those 'real' people whom they write about – this very dichotomy is based on an explanatory logic. It is based upon the logic of 'the integral pedagogicisation of society' (Rancière 1991a, p. 133). This is so because when one accuses researchers in academia of missing the mark of the real on account of being out of touch, such an accusation is itself only an attribute of the larger explanatory assumption that society *could* actually be explained with perfect clarity if only the researcher could just stay in touch. As noted, social arbitrariness is that which an explanatory society wants to refute just as vehemently as linguistic arbitrariness. Following the logic of explanation, academic discourse is always on the right *path* because it is endeavouring to explain the order of things. Academic discourse may not *arrive* at explaining the order of things, but that is a different matter. If it does not arrive, that is because it has been too long away from the 'real.' In a society pedagogicized, academic discourse cannot be wrong. It can only be out of out of touch. That the political philosophy of recognition might be out of touch is thus not the point here.

RECOGNITION WITHOUT TEACHERS?

So far, we have used a pedagogical lens to illustrate the difference between Rancière's understanding of politics, on the one hand, and the politics of recognition, on the other. In particular, we have looked at the debate about recognition that has been going on between recognition's two major proponents, Nancy Fraser and Axel Honneth. We have shown that this debate is more properly understood as a teaching, a teaching that is itself part of the explanatory order. At this point, it might be objected that the preceding reading of Fraser and Honneth has not made a good enough case against recognition 'itself' because we have simply shown the pitfalls of recognition's teachers. It might be objected that if Fraser and Honneth do not do justice to recognition, someone else might. It might be said that if 'ignorant schoolmasters' were to teach recognition, then recognition itself might remain a fine political option. Or, it might be asked: If recognition had no teacher at all, might it proceed untouched by the explanatory infection, and thus remain a viable political strategy?

One proponent of such a view is Jean-Phillipe Deranty. In his article, 'Jacques Rancière's Contribution to the Ethics of Recognition',

Deranty has argued that there are significant similarities between Rancière's thought and political theories of recognition (2003). Deranty proposes the following as a summary of Rancière's recognitive contribution:

> Rancière's position is that of a critical participant in the ethics of recognition . . . he reminds us of the irreducible fact that human community is structurally based on domination and exploitation. But he also gives us the tools for understanding struggle for recognition as the other irreducible fact of human community. His supple theory of the pragmatic verification of equality makes it well adapted to understand and analyze contemporary social, political, and cultural struggles. (Deranty 2003, p. 153)

Deranty sees in the ethics of recognition a number of structural, intersubjective and linguistic similarities with Rancière's political theorizing. For Deranty, the Hegelian legacy of recognitive struggle leaves contemporary theorists like Habermas and Honneth in theoretical positions that no longer honour Hegel's dialectic thought. As Deranty shows, Habermas and Honneth deal in inadequate ways with the centrality of domination and exploitation in Hegel. 'The appeal of Rancière's political writings lies in the fact that it is a type of ethics of recognition, but one that also deals seriously with the phenomena of domination and exploitation, putting them at the conceptual heart of theory' (Deranty 2003, p. 150). Rancière's logic 'is closer to the spirit of Hegelian dialectic than its heirs apparent, in that it puts alienation and scission at the heart of every (would-be) reconciled moment' (Deranty 2003, p. 150).

It is possible both to agree and disagree with Deranty. For example, Deranty is surely correct when he likens recognitive theory to Rancière's political thought since each insists that politics is born out of struggle and disagreement. However, Deranty is surely incorrect when he likens them because in each case 'language is the medium in which the denial of recognition becomes manifest and through which the struggle for recognition is often fought' (Deranty 2003, p. 147). Such a claim fails to understand Rancière's account of language in its arbitrariness. In the work of Rancière, the 'forest of signs' is far from being a medium, or a tool. Language is not a medium for human beings to use in an instrumental way to attain a more transcendent, non-linguistic, form of the good life. These are simple, and certainly incomplete, examples of how one might agree or disagree with Deranty.

But to agree or disagree, as we have just done, with Deranty about the nuances of Rancière's thought as being commensurate or incommensurate with recognitive thought, such agreeing or disagreeing gets one nowhere. To agree or disagree on this matter is already to enact the sort of will to order that is enacted by one who practices the explanation of political philosophy. By agreeing or disagreeing on such a truth, one acts, once again, as a master explicator. Doing so, one demonstrates comparison and contrast, one shows and tells, and one brings depth to the surface. One partakes in 'a discourse that separates truth from illusion' (Rancière 2006a, p. 10). In fact, any supposed exercise in setting the record straight about Rancière and recognition cannot be easily separated from the explanatory logic of the teaching of recognition. When one enters a conversation about recognition, one inevitably enters into a conversation with those who explain the logic of recognition. Thus, one converses using an explanatory logic. The language of explanation can only be answered by the language of explanation.

Indeed, this is precisely Rancière's insight on the societal role of explanatory logic, or, to say the same thing, the societal role of pedagogical logic, or 'society pedagogicized' (Rancière 1991, p. 133). Explanation is not only a logic for teachers who teach. While Fraser and Honneth can be singled out as master explicators of recognition, it is not only *their* thinking that is circumscribed by the logic of explanation. Anyone who attempts to join the conversation of political philosophy is likely to be caught up in its will to order. This is also another way to say that a critique of Fraser and Honneth is not a critique of their work being too academic and thus out of touch with 'real' people. It is not only academic work that is circumscribed by the logic of explanation. The logic of explanation is a social logic. It is not only a logic of certain teachers, nor only a logic of academic researchers. It is more broadly the logic of an orientation towards how one should arrive at the truth that is supposed to set one free. And when one attempts to arrive at a truth like the truth of recognition, one is quickly mired in the explanatory logic that guides the thinking of political philosophy.

Thus, Rancière's educational thinking informs political philosophy by reminding all who engage in the discourse on recognition that there is no view from nowhere, and there is indeed a specific way that one is required to engage when one engages in such a discourse. When Rancière criticizes political philosophy for trying to give order to the arbitrariness of social life, it is should not be forgotten that such order is established in a certain way. One learns this certain way by paying attention to the movement of stultifying pedagogy. It is not enough to say that order is established by means of creating inequality in the name of equality. It is not enough to say that the order is established by creating hierarchy in the name of egalitarianism. It is not enough to say that the sensible is established by a partitioning of the sensible into a sensible where some are heard and others have no part. When one says such things, one implies that inequality, hierarchy and the partitioning of the sensible are somehow established 'out there' or by 'the powers that be'. On the contrary, order is established – in all its inequality, its hierarchy, and its sensibility – in an explanatory way. That is to say, it is established in a way that is as common as the work of teachers and researchers, but is not limited to the work of teachers and researchers. When order is thus established, it is not possible to answer order in terms that are other than explanatory. This means that when one tries to prove that Rancière's thinking is, or is not, commensurate with the struggle for recognition, one cannot step outside the police order to do so. One must proceed by explaining. To say that Rancière's thinking offers 'a type of ethics of recognition' is to police Rancière's thinking (Deranty 2003, p. 150). There is, then, no truth of recognition that might be proven to be commensurate or incommensurate with Rancière's thought. Or, there may be such a truth, but such a truth can only be found through the logic of explication. In such a case, there will be a truth. But as is the case with all explanatory truths, it will not be a truth that sets one free. It will not be a truth that helps one to get anywhere significant, or that leads to some progress other than an explanatory progress.

CHAPTER 6

TRUTH IN EDUCATION, TRUTH IN EMANCIPATION

> Truth is not told. It is whole, and language fragments it; it is necessary, and languages are arbitrary. It was this thesis on the arbitrariness of languages – even more than the proclamation of universal teaching – that made Jacotot's teaching scandalous.
>
> (Rancière 1991a, p. 60)

INTRODUCTION

Education is commonly described in one of three ways. These ways roughly correspond to the traditional, progressive and critical models of education. As a traditional project, education is conceived as a platform for disseminating a common set of learnings. These learnings will, in turn, enable citizens to share a common language for use in the public sphere. Such learnings may or may not derive from the experiences of the student since traditional education is not concerned with the private lives that students have had in the past, but with the common knowledge that needs to be fostered so that they can speak with others in the public sphere. Progressive education shares the same liberalist tendencies of traditional theory, but progressives are more concerned about the bridge to be constructed between private experience and public life. So while the progressive orientation shares the desire to create a common body of knowledge that will enable the communication of citizens in the public sphere, progressives insist that a common body of knowledge can only be understood from the particular experience of each particular person. Thus, one must link private experience to public discourse. From the critical point of view, both the traditional and progressive accounts fall short. Instead, education itself is identified as a tool that has been used by the state to foster inequality. Education must be changed so that it no longer serves hegemony. Education must be re-fashioned so that it no longer impedes democracy, emancipation and enlightenment.

These three orientations also have different assumptions about the status of truth and its relation to education. While each is indeed part of an Enlightenment orientation towards truth; that is to say, while each construes truth to be an attainable educational goal, each offers a different version of truth's relation to education. Following the traditional model of using direct instruction to expose students to a common body of knowledge, education transports the student from where he or she is, presently, towards the true. The true is where the student must arrive. It is the common language to be shared. The true is what one must be exposed to through direct instruction. From the progressive perspective, the truth is to be shared by all, but it must be shared in a pragmatic way, in a way that speaks to experience. Progressives are generally aligned with William James's famous statement on truth's pragmatics, that truth is an idea 'upon which we can ride' (2009). In other words, the truths to be learned through education need to be grounded in the particular experience of each person if they are to be successfully used (as opposed to merely passively understood) in community. Following the critical perspective, education can neither bring students to the true by direct instruction, nor can it do so by appealing to experience. The truth isn't so easy to attain because it is hidden behind a veil of ideological obfuscation. When schools categorize people and create hierarchies, when they educate some students better than others, they usually do so in a way that covers up what they are actually doing. Truth is actually to be found in the ideological and structural inequalities that privilege some people and oppress others. The critical project is thus to remove the façade of education, whether that façade be traditional or progressive, so that the truth of power and oppression can be exposed.

Notably, though, none of these three dominant approaches to education has an orientation towards truth that is *educationally* grounded. What is meant by this is that each of these three approaches to education – the traditional, the progressive, and the critical – imports an orientation towards truth that is grounded in non-educational thinking. All three have a view of truth that stems from Enlightenment, objectivist thought. Traditionalism has a view of truth that comes straight out of the Enlightenment's concern for a public space that each individual can share in. Progressivism shares the same view, but with an added concern for the experience and psychological development of the child. The critical orientation towards truth comes primarily from the philosophy of Marx, and shares with traditionalism and progressivism what might be called a vehicular understanding of truth in education. That is to say, critical educational theory, like the traditional and the progressive, presumes that education can *move* the student so that he or she *arrives* at the truth. But in the case of criticalism, the veil of ideological obfuscation must be removed before education can transport the student to truth. These orientations, while deeply important for thinking in various ways about truth vis-à-vis education, do not consider the status of truth *as a function of education*. The dominant approaches to education do not consider what education itself might teach us about the status of truth therein. They do not entertain the possibility that education might present a metaphor for truth. They each import a version of truth that is, in essence, foreign to the workings of education itself.

In this chapter, we will first employ the work of Rancière to offer an educational understanding of truth that comes from *within* education. By this, we do not mean that it is an educational thinker, namely Rancière, who has come up with this understanding of truth (although it is). Nor do we mean that we will offer some truth about what education does or does not do (though we believe that we will). Nor do we mean that we will be able to say which perspective on truth – the traditional, progressive, critical or the one we will elaborate – is the truest (though one might assert it is the latter). What we mean is that we will investigate how education fosters a certain understanding of truth through the ways that things are taught and learned, as well as through the general social role of the school. Education thus provides a metaphor for truth; and by doing so, it offers an explanation of truth. But as we will show, Rancière refutes this educational metaphor for truth at the same time that he shows its workings. He favours instead a more agnostic version of truth that does *not* normally get promulgated by education. We will also map Rancière's agnostic account of truth onto his 'new logic' of emancipation. As will be shown, an agnostic relation to truth shows itself more fundamental to Rancière's emancipatory logic than one might expect.

PEDAGOGY'S EXPLANATORY ROLE

Arguably, Rancière's most important contribution to educational theory lies not in the more obvious description of universal teaching one finds in *The Ignorant Schoolmaster*, but in his attention to the form of the school in the context of Western democracies and Western political philosophy. The importance of this contribution can be re-stated succinctly by saying that the school, and by extension pedagogy in general, has a function that commonly goes unnoticed in educational theory. It has an *explanatory* function. That is to say, the school does something by the very fact of being a school at the same time that it affords an opportunity for teaching and learning. The school *continues* on the model described in Plato's *Republic*. The republic

> is a city in which legislation is entirely resumed in education – education, however going beyond the simple instruction of the schoolmaster and being offered at any moment of the day in the chorus of what is visually and aurally up for grabs. (Rancière 1999, p. 68)

The republic runs smoothly because it establishes schools that explain an 'archipolitical' order (Rancière 1999, p. 65). The school, in Western democracies, continues this explanatory function. It thus has a double role according to Rancière. The school not only educates citizens – whether that education be traditional, progressive, or critical. It also *performs, in* the arena of knowledge, an ordering that echoes the political ordering of society. As Rancière points out, '. . . the idea of a master who transmits knowledge to a student or a learner who is in front of the master, and who doesn't know something, this idea is in reality a cosmology and not simply a method' (Rancière 2004b). The school gives order by performing *explanations*.

It might seem, at first glance, that certain forms of education do not, or at least need not, partake in this explanatory paradigm that is denounced by Rancière. That is, it might seem that some methodologies are less explanatory than others, and thus less a part of this 'working allegory' that has directed the school ever since Plato's *Republic*. For example, it might be argued that progressive education, with its condemnation of traditional methods, is none other than a condemnation of the detrimental effects of too much explanation. This seems to be the case with John Dewey's critique of traditionalism. Dewey, after all, is concerned with creating educational situations that are less about 'verbal methods' and more about direct experience (Dewey 1910, p. 178). He is critical of traditional education's focus on abstract linguistic symbols, and instead advocates a return to practice. Noting his disgust with traditional education in *Democracy and Education*, Dewey remarks that educators not only explain, but even when they know that explanation is wrongheaded, they *explain* its wrongheadedness without sensing the irony of this double explanation:

> That education is not an affair of 'telling' and being told, but an active and constructive process, is a principle almost as generally violated in practice as conceded in theory. Is not this deplorable situation due to the fact that the doctrine is itself merely told? It is preached; it is lectured; it is written about. (Dewey 1916, p. 38)

So it might seem that progressive education is well aware of the pitfalls of explanation, and that its major spokesperson aims to establish a method that is not explanatory.

However, Dewey's polemics against traditional education, as well as his extended efforts to establish a progressive movement in education that would not be explanatory, are themselves part of an explanatory pedagogy. Dewey explains how human beings learn, he explains how traditional education is full of faults, and he explains how educators might better organize curriculum and instruction in order to improve teaching and learning. Dewey actually enacts the ironic double explanation that he condemns in others. This is the lesson one draws from Rancière's account of the school's explanatory function: There cannot be a method of education that does *not* partake in the explanatory order of sociality. As soon as any form of education becomes a method, then it will, by virtue of being a method, be an explanation of how human beings learn, and what they should learn. As soon as any form of education becomes a method, then it becomes a 'school' in four senses of the word. It becomes a school in the sense that it establishes a practice that has followers. It becomes a school in the sense that it creates the circumstances for a number of students to be educated in a similar way. It becomes a school in the platonic sense that it establishes an orderly body of knowledge that contributes to the social order. And, it becomes a school in the jacotist sense that it reaffirms the explanatory order of knowledge acquisition. So it does not matter that progressive pedagogy ostensibly advocates a non-explanatory form of education. Progressivism partakes in the explanatory social order by offering a method, a method that cannot help becoming a school.

It might seem, too, that critical education is not explanatory because it offers an explicit critique of explanation. Freire, for example,

Freire

criticizes traditional pedagogy for engaging in the oppressive psychic dynamics of over-explaining. For Freire, when things are too much explained, the one-explaining obtains a structural superiority over the one-explained-to. This is precisely the 'banking' situation. In such a situation, the Hegelian dynamic of master and slave sets in. The one-explained-to lives vicariously through the words of the one-explaining: 'What characterizes the oppressed is their subordination to the consciousness of the master' (Freire 1970, p. 31). As the oppressor narrates, the listeners become 'beings for another' (Freire 1970, p. 31). This psychic dynamic gets established precisely because there is too much explaining done in traditional education, and not enough dialogue happening. As students are explained-to, they become divided and alienated. Freire notes that

> the conflict lies in the choice between being wholly themselves or being divided; between ejecting the oppressor within or not ejecting them; between human solidarity or alienation; between following prescriptions or having choices; between being spectators or actors; between acting or having the illusion of acting through the action of the oppressors. (Freire 1970, p. 30)

Students do not act for themselves under the banking system because they are too busy listening to what is being explained to them. 'Students are not called upon to know, but to memorize the contents narrated by the teacher' (Freire 1970, p. 61).

In Freire's case, too, it is ironic that the critical method of problem-posing education necessarily gets introduced in the form of *explanation*. Explanations, such as the following, are commonplace in Freire's *Pedagogy of the Oppressed*:

> Through dialogue, the teacher-of-the-students and the students-of-the-teacher cease to exist and a new term emerges: teacher-student with students-teachers. The teacher is no longer merely the-one-who-teaches, but one who is himself taught in dialogue with the students, who in turn while being taught also teach. (Freire 1970, p. 161)

Thus, in spite of the fact that problem-posing education presents itself in the form of an antidote to narration, the theory expounded by Freire is a *narrated* theory. It is explained. Explained in a way true to the form of the school. In spite of critical education's best spokesman's best efforts to offer a method that eschews explanation, Freire own method suffers from the very narrative sickness that he condemns in banking education.

It is interesting to note that even traditional education claims to eschew explanation to some extent. Traditional education describes itself today as an antidote to the endless explanations of progressivism and criticalism (see Hirsch 1999; Ravitch 1995). According to this traditional reaction to progressive and critical education, there is currently too much explaining going on. Progressive and critical education both go to great lengths to describe the experiential, social and cultural backgrounds of students. They do so with the avowed intent to *correct for* inequalities so that the educational playing field can be levelled. From a traditional perspective, this is an explanatory waste of time. One must *not* take a detour through the current socio-cultural situations of students. One must *not* do such elaborate explaining. Why? Because the school is supposed to establish a *new* idiom for each student, a public idiom that need not be prepared for, because it does not depend upon the out-of-school circumstances of the student. From the traditional perspective, there will be enough explanation done *anyway* as the student is taught such a public idiom. There is no need to wallow in the *added* explanation of the dismal circumstances of the oppressed. The oppressed know their own circumstances. Such circumstances need no added explanation. So traditional education admits to partaking in the explanatory order all the while refuting an *excess* of explanation. Traditional teaching explains, but not too much.

EXPLANATION, LANGUAGE AND TRUTH

In concert with the *educational* perspective on truth that we are proposing in this chapter, let us use Rancière's work to shift the matter of explanation onto the terrain of truth. To make this shift, it is necessary to understand the essential connection between the explanatory order and truth itself. For, when one uses explanation, one assumes that truth can be arrived at by a sequence of propositional statements. During explanation, one uses language to present the truth. One establishes a certain linguistic relation with truth. When one uses language to explain something, one draws a direct line from the word to truth, from the word that explains, to the truth of the thing explained. For Rancière, this direct line from language to truth is the basis of an explanatory folly that drives every form of the school. The propensity to explain ignores a central aspect of language, an aspect that Rancière emphasizes in many of his writings, not only in his educational work – that language is arbitrary. Because language is arbitrary, one can never draw a direct line from the word to truth. 'Truth is not told', writes Rancière,

> It is whole, and language fragments it; it is necessary, and languages are arbitrary. It was this thesis on the arbitrariness of languages – even more than the proclamation of universal teaching – that made Jacotot's teaching scandalous. (Rancière 1991a, p. 60)

The folly of the school is that it misconstrues the relation between language and truth. This is because the school misconstrues the arbitrary nature of language.

To more clearly understand the folly of the school, that is to say, the educational/explanatory relation to truth, it is useful to juxtapose it more fully to its opposite – language's arbitrary relation to truth. Rancière's work in political theory, in aesthetics, as well as in education is committed to this understanding of language's arbitrary nature, and thus to language's incommensurable relation to the truth. In political theory, Rancière posits the arbitrary nature of language as an 'unreality of representation' (1995a, p. 51). This is to say that language cannot directly represent reality. It cannot say truth. But far from being disappointed with the arbitrariness of language, Rancière uses representation's unreality as a hopeful point of departure for those who would truly aspire to participate in a democratic order. Thus, 'the democratic man' is 'a being capable of embracing a distance between words and things that is not deception, not trickery, but humanity' (Rancière 1995a, p. 51). So while language is too arbitrary to access truth directly, this fact is not cause for dismay for one who would participate in a true democracy, it is instead a point of hope for such a person. That language is arbitrary means that there is always hope to reconfigure the sensible. If language were not arbitrary, if words were already fixed to truth, then there would be no chance for human beings to insert themselves *differently* into the sensible's distribution. There would be no opportunity for subjectification. Thus, the arbitrariness of language

> turns both every utterance and every reception into an adventure which presupposes the tense interaction of two wishes: a wish to say

and a wish to hear, each threatened at every moment by the danger of falling into the abyss of distraction, above which is stretched the tightrope of a will to meaning. (Rancière 1995a, p. 81)

People certainly ignore the arbitrariness of language's relation to the truth. But in doing so they ignore the possibility of true democratic interaction that reconfigures the social order.

Rancière goes so far as to say that each person who participates in politics, as opposed to 'policing', actually acknowledges, either wittingly or unwittingly, this arbitrariness of language. For, the person who participates in politics knows that language has two levels: one that ostensibly connects language directly to truth, and one that proves just the opposite, that language is not fixed to truth. The second level of language is invoked every time a political subject acknowledges that the terms for understanding another are subject to redistribution rather than being fixed. Thus,

> In any social discussion in which there is actually something to discuss, this structure is implicated, a structure in which the place, the object, and the subjects of discussion are themselves in dispute and must in the first instance be tested. (Rancière 1999, p. 55)

The political actor is not a person who takes language to be fixed to truth. Rather, such an actor is one who understands that utterances are always contestable rather than tethered to particular truths. The political actor has 'this second-degree understanding' (Rancière 1999, p. 46). Such an understanding entails 'the constitution of a specific speech scene in which it is a matter of constructing another relationship by making the position of the enunciator explicit' (Rancière 1999, p. 46). The political actor knows that language is arbitrary, and he or she will make such arbitrariness understood.

Rancière also insists that the arbitrariness of language makes poets of those who would accept its arbitrariness. 'The democratic man is a being who speaks, which is also to say a poetic being', writes Rancière in *On the Shores of Politics* (Rancière 1995a, p. 51). This is so because one who accepts the arbitrariness of language, yet who goes on to communicate certain truths nevertheless, such a person must engage in the sort of translation that is both the joy and the burden of the artist. The artist knows how difficult yet necessary it is to convey truths that one takes to be universal, yet that have never been precisely articulated before. The poet works 'in the gap between the silent language of emotion and the arbitrariness of the spoken tongue' (Rancière 1991a, p. 68). Yet this is no different than the work of any reasonable being who must struggle with the arbitrariness of language in an effort to convey one's thoughts to another.

> Each one of us is an artist to the extent that he carries out a double process; he is not content to be a mere journeyman but wants to make all work a means of expression, and he is not content to feel something but tries to impart it to others. (Rancière 1991a, p. 70)

When one conveys one's thoughts to others through language, one must give order, anew, to a handful of signs. These signs will form a work that will be interpreted by another. This order-giving, this work, and this interpretation, indicate the extent to which *each* person is an artist.

Once again, only this time in an artistic sense, an insistence on language's arbitrariness is cause for celebration rather than remorse. This is because language's arbitrariness pushes the poet to *demonstrate* his or her confidence in the *commonality* of human experience, a demonstration that will be cobbled out in spite of language's inadequacies. While language is not *naturally* attached to this or that truth, the poet attempts to translate truth from one person's experience to the experience of an interpreter, all the while knowing that language is never up to the task of such a translation. Language is thus seen to be arbitrary in the sense that it is not fixed directly to truth, but this does not mean that language is destined to be the solitary assignation of one's own personal, and random, experience. The poet 'strives to say everything, knowing that everything cannot be said, but that it is the unconditional tension of the translator that opens the possibility of the other tension, the other will' (Rancière 1991a, pp. 69–70). Thus 'we understand what Racine has to tell us, that his thoughts are not different from ours, and that his expressions are only achieved by our counter-translation' (Rancière 1991a, p. 70). The poet asks us to prove, through our own translation of the work, that while language may be arbitrary, it can still be cause for a commonality based on the translations and counter-translations of the poet and those who read the poem.

Truth in Education

Determined to separate itself from political actors and poets who *do* understand language's arbitrariness is the school in all its forms. The school as it generally functions cannot allow that language's arbitrariness to be exposed because such exposure would undermine its explanatory teachings on truth. For education to function smoothly, and for its various methods to be employed according to the latest innovative research, truth must be accessible through language. It cannot be the case that 'truth is not told. It is whole, and language fragments it, it is necessary, and languages are arbitrary' (Rancière 1991a, p. 60). If such were the case, then the school would be relegated to an unhappy mutism. Neither could subject matter be explained, nor could there be explanations of how to avoid, how to make experiential, or how to demystify, explanations of subject matter. It cannot be the case that 'truth settles no conflict in the public place' (Rancière 1991a, p. 90). If this were the case, then the pedagogical improvements that are recounted *ad nauseam* in newspapers and in journals would need to be stricken from record. On the contrary, the school must, and does, teach something about truth, something that keeps the school apart from political actors and poets. The school must explain things, thus demonstrating that truth is accessible through language, and that folly resides not in front of this curtain but behind it. The school, because it is believed to be the most effective place for teaching and learning to happen, stands as proof positive that the truth can be explained and that language is not arbitrary.

As Rancière correctly indicates, it is not difficult to educate in an explanatory fashion. Thus the school constantly reaffirms the distance between its own success, on the one hand, and the potential 'anarchy of the democratic circulation of knowledge' created by an arbitrary relation between language and truth, on the other (Rancière, 1999, p. 69) 'There are a hundred ways to instruct, and learning also takes place in the stultifier's school . . . One always learns when listening to someone speak' (Rancière 1991a, p. 102). To put this a bit differently, it is not the case that language's arbitrariness *prevents* the success of explanatory education. Rather, the explanatory school sets the stage for its own success at the same time that it repeatedly introduces explanation as the prime mover of any social organism that deserves to be called a school. Indeed, the explanatory regime of education can't lose, and this for two reasons. First, it 'becomes the normal regime under which the explicatory institution is rationalized and justified' (Rancière 1991a, p. 122). That is, education is deemed successful not only when it has explained well, but *because* it has explained well. Secondly, neither language's arbitrariness, nor an *awareness of* language's arbitrariness, can get in the way of explanatory justification precisely because neither *proves* anything about any sort of truth, including the particular educational truths that are 'rationalized and justified' by the regime of explanatory education (Rancière 1991a, p. 122).

What can be noticed in Rancière's work is thus an educational reversal of the way truth is to be understood. Earlier, the traditional, progressive, and critical orientations toward truth were described. It was claimed that these orientations, while differing from one another, could happily be placed under the more general Enlightenment understanding of an education that functions as a vehicle to transport the student to truth. Actually, this earlier description neglects to observe that truth's status might be immanent, rather than transcendent, to education. Thus the very way we explained education's relation to truth should be understood as mistaken. We assumed, from the onset, that truth is something 'out there', something usefully considered from a philosophical perspective, and we assumed that such a consideration could lead to some valid conclusions about truth's relation to education. But one might have paused at such a moment to consider Rancière's words: 'As for the truth, it doesn't rely on philosophers who say they are its friend: it is only friends with itself' (Rancière 1991a, p. 60). Describing truth in relation to education disregards the fact that explanatory education itself establishes the practices that underwrite such a description. After all, one must be educated in order to have such a way of describing truth. And here, 'being educated' does not mean that one must have been to school for a number of years. It means rather that one has been inducted into an explanatory way of understanding the world which assumes that language is not arbitrary, that language rather establishes direct lines to truth. In this case, lines to the truth of truth.

No form of education has a vehicular relation to the truth. Rather, education itself, as an explanatory form of social order, compels one to talk about truth in such a way. One might rather expect that it is philosophy which compels one to seek answers about fundamental human concerns such as truth, and that educational philosophy compels one to seek answers about such fundamental educational concerns as truth's relation to education. While it might be the case that truth is a concern of philosophy, it is the school, in its explanatory form, which sends one on a linguistic quest to get at the status of truth. In this sense, the school is a much more basic philosophical sort of training than philosophy itself. By this, we do not mean that one should go to school in order to be educated enough to study philosophical questions like 'What is the status of truth'? Indeed, it is the logic of the explanatory order that makes such an 'educated-enough-for-philosophy' notion understandable.

Truth as a concept to investigate is in fact a prime example of the double gambit of the explanatory order of education. Even while truth's linguistic accessibility is a *sine qua non* of the explanatory order, even while this accessibility is assumed, and taught, in the most 'elementary' sorts of teachings; nevertheless, truth, as a concept, is assigned to the curriculum of only those most 'advanced' students who study philosophy. In such a regime, the most basic of questions must answer to the retardation of explanation's lengthy order of events. The school teaches one suppositions about truth at the most elementary of levels. The study of these basic suppositions is relegated to some distant future.

Immanent Text

Rancière instead presents us with an account of truth that is immanent to education. It is an account of the explanatory regime's confidence in the linguistic accessibility of facts, opinions, feelings, ideas, logics, and narratives. It is the account of a regime that would have (only) philosophers worrying about the status of truth, yet would promulgate a linguistic confidence in the ability to learn truth at even the most 'elementary' levels. It does not matter whether such an ability is fostered by traditional, progressive or critical methods. A language-to-truth perspective is immanent to each of these schools. Of course, this perspective on truth is not *Rancière's* perspective. If truth's presentation is immanent to education, it is not immanent to the sort of education that Rancière advocates in the figure of Jacotot and his universal teaching. Rancière's own presentation of truth in pedagogy demonstrates that universal teaching will have no truck with truth that is explainable. He makes this demonstration through vivid descriptions of truth such as the ones that follow: 'Each one of us describes our own parabola around the truth. No two orbits are alike. And this is why the explicators endanger our revolution'

(Rancière 1991a, p. 59). 'But for all that, truth is not foreign to us, and we are not exiled from its country' (Rancière 1991a, 58) 'The experience of veracity attaches us to its absent center; it makes us circle around its foyer' (Rancière 1991a, p. 58). Truth is a planet whose 'territory' the emancipated person can only approach, and only in his or her particular way. There will never be a landing, and certainly not a landing that can be explained.

So Rancière's own perspective on truth is connected to his understanding of the arbitrariness of language, upon language's inability to access truth directly. On the flip side of this linguistic non-approachability of truth, stands Rancière's presentation of truth itself, and of truth's indifference to people: 'Truth doesn't bring people together at all. It is not given to us. It exists independently from us and does not submit to our piecemeal sentences' (Rancière 1991a, p. 58). And to repeat, 'Truth settles no conflict in the public place' (Rancière 1991a, p. 90). Such an agnostic understanding of truth once again underscores the folly of explanation. For, our piecemeal sentences cannot explain the truth no matter how much we might want them to. This is why the quintessential explanatory sentence is at once altogether common, and altogether mistaken. This quintessential sentence, 'Do you understand?' is altogether common in educational situations, that is, in explanatory situations. Yet, it is altogether mistaken as it presents truth as 'given to us', as something that needs only to be understood through explanation. As Rancière points out in *Disagreement*, the master's question 'Do you understand?' hides the fact that there are circumstances that enact the very say-ability of 'Do you understand'? To answer either 'I do understand', or 'I do not understand', to this question is thus to accept the social terms that confer say-ability on such a question (Rancière 1999, pp. 45–47; see also Chapter 3, this volume). Truth that *is* given to us loves such a question. Whether the answer to the question is 'yes' or 'no' is no matter. Either way, the truth's terms are already conferred upon the answer. Rancière's understanding of truth, however, would always throw such a question into question. It would problematize even this most commonplace of sentences.

TRUTH AND EMANCIPATION

But why truth? Why would one focus on truth, or on Rancière's educational rendition of truth? The obvious answer would be that truth is a venerable philosophical theme to explore, that sound theories of truth are always philosophically important. In this spirit, an essay on truth is an essay quite suited for a chapter in a book devoted to a philosopher such as Jacques Rancière. After all, there are many philosophical volumes that have been devoted to the theme of truth. The answer to this question, 'Why truth?', should not be so easily disciplined, however. We should have already learned from Rancière that academic discourses such as the philosophical discourse on truth, that such discourses serve the explanatory order. Such discourses do discipline rather than liberate. Against the backdrop of a facile disciplinary answer, we might return instead to Rancière's comments on the 'interventionist' quality of his work:

> his books [and here Rancière is referring to himself in the third person] are always forms of intervention in specific contexts. He never intended to produce a theory of politics, aesthetics, literature, cinema or anything else. He thinks that there is already a good deal of them and he loves trees enough to avoid destroying them to add one more theory to all those available on the market. (Rancière 2009a, p. 114)

In fact, our particular intervention on truth does not oblige itself to the venerable tradition of epistemology in philosophy. We are not simply trying to elucidate Rancière's particular theory of truth. We are *not* doing so precisely because such an elucidation is not in keeping with the fact that Rancière, as he himself says, is not intending to establish another theory of truth. Rather, we are introducing truth for two purposes. First, for the purpose encountered above, that is, as an intervention on the supposed ameliorative role of the school. We have shown that, through the form of the school, truth wrongly serves as a linguistic accessibility, as an endpoint supposedly reachable through explanatory language. In fact, the school does not get us to truth through its explanations. Instead, it, itself, produces the supposed efficacy of its explanatory form. The school explains that truth needs to be explained.

The second purpose of this intervention on truth is to further an account of emancipation. Emancipation, as we have argued, has had an educational logic historically linked to Enlightenment thought as exemplified in the work of Immanuel Kant. We have noted that this legacy of emancipatory logic has been characterized by three assumptions, each of which Rancière's project of emancipation counters: that emancipation is done *to* somebody, that there is a fundamental inequality between the emancipator and the one to be emancipated, and that the experiences of the one to be emancipated are distrusted. Too, we have noted that the school has been historically posited as a method for bringing people, especially children, to the point where they become emancipated. In fact, the form of emancipation is reflected in, and reflects, the form of the school. Emancipation is said to be achieved through the process of schooling, and, the process of schooling can be seen to carry the assumptions of emancipation. Now, given the *explanatory* nature of the school, and given the school's metaphorical role of explaining the importance of explaining, one can notice a few equivalences between the trope and practice of explanation, and the logic of emancipation of the Kantian legacy. Explanation is structurally equivalent to this logic of emancipation in at least three ways: Explanation is done *to* someone, explanation assumes an inequality between the explicator and the one to whom things are explained, and explanation discounts the experiences of the one to whom things are explained. In this sense, the school not only constantly explains the importance of explanation, but it also constantly explains the centrality of explanation to emancipation. The school explains itself and it also explains that emancipation explains.

It is necessary to go further though. For there is a connection between emancipation and truth that derives from this emancipatory habit of explanation. Or rather, there is a connection between emancipation and truth that derives from this *non*-emancipatory habit of explanation. The connection is simple really. It is also a connection that motivates our investigation into Rancière's presentation of truth. Such motivation is not borne out of any philosophical reverence for truth. Indeed, the exact opposite is true. The connection is borne out the profound irreverence for truth that we have been detailing above. Actually, the connection between truth and emancipation is more of a non-connection than a connection, yet it is a central connection nevertheless. The connection between emancipation and truth rests in Rancière's simple, yet emphatic, declarations that truth is *not* connected to the discursive life of human beings. Truth is thus *not* connected to the words, thoughts and acts that bring about emancipation. 'Truth is not told. It is whole, and language fragments it; it is necessary, and languages are arbitrary'

125

(Rancière 1991a, p. 60). 'Truth settles no conflict in the public space' (Rancière 1991a, p. 90). 'As for the truth, it doesn't rely on philosophers who say they are its friend: it is only friends with itself' (Rancière 1991a, p. 60). 'Each one of us describes our own parabola around the truth. No two orbits are alike. And this is why the explicators endanger our revolution' (Rancière 1991a, p. 59). These statements and others offer an emphatic *dis*-connection between the words, thoughts and acts that bring about emancipation, on the one hand, and, on the other hand, truth. The relation between truth and emancipation, rather than being a connection, is a widely accepted conceit. It is a conceit that recommends an explanatory detour, a detour beginning from the oppressed person, moving through the truth, then returning back to the person who will have found liberty as a result of having found truth. It is a conceit that encourages an explanatory stultification as one must always first visit the realm of truth before returning home to find liberty.

Such a conceit is detailed at length in Rancière's criticisms of the work of Pierre Bourdieu and Jean-Claude Passeron (Rancière 2002; Rancière 2003a; Pelletier 2009). Rancière shows how, in their books *The Inheritors* and *Reproduction*, Bourdieu and Passeron produce an analysis of the school that sets up sociological truth as the *only* truth that will enable the educational practitioner to enact a liberating pedagogy (Bourdieu and Passeron 1979; 1977). So following Rancière's analysis, these works should be read as establishing the following conceit: An instructor *must* take the sociological road to arrive at educational truths. Only by arriving at such truths will the instructor get to the point where he or she will be able to understand what it means to practice liberating pedagogy. Writes Rancière,

> where are we to find the hidden in this scissoring of statistics and opinion, this immense chattering of demystification where *truth* [our emphasis] cannot be distinguished from its imitation? 'The particular difficulty [Rancière now quoting Bourdieu and Passeron] of sociology comes from the fact that it teaches things that everybody knows in a way, but which they don't want to know or cannot know because the law of the system is to hide those things from them'. (Rancière 2003a, p. 170)

Thus in the work of the sociologist, Rancière discerns a most obvious conceit. The sociologist explains that it is in sociology's nature to

reveal truths that can only be arrived at through sociological explanation. With regard to liberatory education, one must first study sociology
in order to be able to understand 'the law of the system' of education. One must take a detour through truth, because common sense
will never lead one to the point where one can discern truth from
imitation. Of course, Rancière goes a bit further in his criticism of
Bourdieu and Passeron. He notes that their later work actually adds
a disparaging twist to their own earlier conceit. For, ultimately they
show how liberatory education is almost impossible, even if the
teacher has successfully become aware of the sociological truths
of the educational system. This is so because the teacher is, him or
herself, inevitably part of the production of social capital that is
made so obvious through the research of the sociologist. So even
when it is the sociologist's role to show that emancipation is *not* possible, it is still the case that one must first arrive at a sociological
insight in order to reconcile oneself to such an impossibility.

But the sociologist is only one thinker among many, many others
to establish the conceit of a truth that will set one free (or perhaps *not*
set one free). The example of Bourdieu and Passeron serves as a
place-marker for a more general tendency to order the progress of
thought, to keep thought from thinking about liberty too soon.
It serves as an example of the schoolish habit of setting students
on a detour through truth before they are said to be ready for emancipation. The example of the sociologist is just a bit more ironic than
others since the sociologist claims to be showing the way toward the
truth of emancipation at the same time that he or she is making
emancipation all the more distant.

But all is not of critique and irony in Rancière's work on truth and
emancipation. One can trace the *dis*-connection between truth and
emancipation in a more positive way, in a way that shows Rancière's
alternative to this conceit. To do so, one can look to the way that
truth's status as a *separate* entity, an entity that humans cannot
adequately represent, guides both political emancipation and pedagogical emancipation in Rancière's work. In other words, the fact
that 'truth settles no conflict in the public space', and the fact that
'truth is not told', is central to Rancière's own logic of emancipation
as this logic pertains to both politics and pedagogy.

Take, for example, that aspect of Rancière's 'new logic' that insists
on an emancipation that trusts (rather than distrusts) the experiences
of the one who is emancipated. Emancipation, according this logic,

127

does *not* occur because the experiences of the one to be emancipated are replaced by a proper and correct understanding. For Rancière, there is on one stage truth, and on another, the linguistic practice of engaging with the world. It is on the latter stage that political emancipation occurs. It is not the case that political emancipation happens outside of the linguistic realm where humans see things, do things, and say things. Emancipation does not happen in some autonomous realm where truth holds sway over the order of things. This might be the case if truth settled conflicts in the public space, if truth could be told and translated perfectly into the state of human affairs. But it is not the case. Language is one thing, and truth is another. Language only 'fragments' truth (Rancière 1991a, p. 60). And it is within language that politics happens. Politics happens within the realm of fragmented truth. It is within language, within truth fragmented, that people are either oppressed or liberated. This is not to say that oppression and liberation are 'merely' linguistic. It is rather to say that they are *indeed* linguistic, and thus have no truck with truth. Emancipation can never be beholden to some proper and correct understanding because emancipation never actually arrives at a proper and correct understanding. Emancipation arrives only at linguistic interventions on the world. It arrives at subjectification, where the distribution of the sensible is reconfigured in ways that enable different configurations of doing, saying, and being. Emancipation happens on one stage while truth happens on another. When the sociologist, or the educator, or anyone else, tries to sell a bill of goods that puts emancipation and truth on the same stage, the sale should be voided. Rancière's new logic of emancipation would refuse such a simplistic connection between truth and political emancipation. It insists that emancipation is fostered in spite of truth rather than by means of truth.

Once again, it is important to state that truth is not being analyzed here on account of its status in philosophical discourse. We are trying instead to link Rancière's agnostic version of truth to emancipation. In fact, one finds that an agnosticism with regard to truth serves as a central concept in Rancière's work on emancipation. A few emancipatory examples from Rancière's work further underscore this fact. One can return first of all to the example of the syllogism created by the French tailors recounted in *On the Shores of Politics*, and noted in our discussion of Rancière's new logic of emancipation (Rancière 1995a). This syllogism, whose major premise was that all people were

equal before the law, and whose minor premise was that these workers should therefore also be equal under the law with regard to their
pay – this syllogism forced a presumption of equality rather than
a demonstration of inequality. Interestingly, the situation created
by the workers' strike has no regard for truth. It takes place on a
discursive level that can only fragment the truth. If there had been
obedience to truth, then the aim of the strike would have been to
prove the evil intent of those who set wages unreasonably low. But
that is not the intent of the strike. The strike is rather intended to
demonstrate the 'beautiful lie' that these workers must be (and here
'must be' should be taken in both its senses) equal with regard to pay
as well as being equal 'under the law' in general (Rancière 2006a,
p. 10). It provides a hypothetical narrative of what is to become
reality in the future rather than a representation of what is true in
the here and now. This syllogism is thus a matter of poetry rather
than a matter of science or truth. It is also a matter of the sorts
of stories that are told by philosophers. The workers' syllogism
enacts a 'beautiful lie' of the same variety that Rancière sees in
Plato's philosophical narratives. Rancière recounts such a beautiful
lie as follows:

> The specificity of the Platonic 'myth' is constituted by the way in
> which it inverts the reasons of knowledge [*savoir*] with the purely
> arbitrary insistence on the story [*conte*]. While the historian and
> the sociologist show us how a certain life produces a certain thought
> expressing a life, the myth of the philosopher refers this necessity
> to an arbitrary 'beautiful lie', a beautiful lie which is at the same
> time the reality of life for the greatest number of people. This
> identity of necessity and contingency, the reality of the lie, cannot
> be rationalized in the form of a discourse which separates truth
> from illusion. It can only be recounted. (Rancière 2006a, p. 10)[1]

The emancipation demonstrated by these French tailors takes place
in spite of truth rather than because of truth. It is demonstrated by
a poetic and philosophical – philosophical in the sense that it tells the
sort of story that a philosopher tells – act that refuses to separate
truth from illusion.[2]

The process of subjectification also serves as an example of the way
that a deliberate agnosticism with regard to truth is central to Rancière's
account of emancipation. As noted earlier, subjectification entails

Subjectification

what Rancière calls 'the production through a series of actions of a body and a capacity for enunciation not previously identifiable within a given field of experience, whose identification is thus part of the reconfiguration of the field of experience' (Rancière 1999, p. 35). But there is a certain weakness that will no doubt have been noted in our presentation of subjectification. Indeed, under close inspection of the way Rancière describes subjectification, it is not easy to understand how subjectification 'actually' happens.[3] It is difficult to know when, where, and how 'the field of experience' is 'reconfigured'. But such a concern over the 'actual' of subjectification is precisely the wrong way to approach the topic, and this is precisely where an agnosticism with regard to truth comes into play. This is not simply to say that one should be agnostic about the 'actual' of subjectification. Such an attitude would merely be avoiding the subject. It is rather to say that subjectification reconfigures the field of experience in the poetic and philosophical senses that we have been describing above. This is to say, subjectification, as a process of reconfiguring the sensible, happens not *in* actuality but *in spite of* actuality. It happens as new speech is forced onto the scene of discourse. This new speech will not have a direct referent in the realm of what is already considered to be true. It is poetic in the sense that poetry exists in spite of, rather than within, what is true. This new speech 'cannot be rationalized in the form of a discourse which separates truth from illusion' (Rancière 2006a, p. 10). And once again, we are not saying that subjectification, as a concept, 'cannot be rationalized in the form of a discourse which separates truth from illusion' (Rancière 2006a, p. 10). On the contrary, one can give concrete examples, such as the French tailors' strike, of subjectification. We are rather saying that subjectification will happen following a narrative that disregards truth, offering its own world instead. This will happen in the same way that the poem and the beautiful lie disregard truth, each offering its own world instead.

And finally we might look to emancipation in education. Here we can again go back to the crucial insistence on the part of Rancière that there must be an 'assumption' of equality of human beings. At first glance, this insistence on assuming seems a bit dubious and a bit arbitrary. Why assume equality? Isn't it simpler to 'actually' believe in the equality of human beings? Why not insist *on* equality rather than on the assumption of equality? With Rancière's agnostic orientation toward truth in mind, however, it becomes quite clear

correspondence/arbitrary

that insisting *on* equality, on equality as a truth, is to situate equality as part of 'a discourse that separates truth from elusion' (Rancière 2006a, p. 10). Yes, the insistence on assuming is indeed arbitrary. It is arbitrary as language is arbitrary. It is arbitrary in the sense that truth 'is necessary, languages are arbitrary' (Rancière 1991a, p. 60). The insistence on assuming is an insistence on telling a beautiful lie that will serve to make sense to a number of people.

In fact, the assumption of equality is just one instance of a more general agnostic attitude toward truth that the emancipatory ped-agogue embraces following the work of Rancière. This attitude can be seen in the various connotations of the word 'ignorant' as it appears in *The Ignorant Schoolmaster*, and then as it appears in Rancière's essay, 'Thinking between disciplines: the aesthetics of knowledge' (2006a), and 'On Ignorant Schoolmasters' (this volume). One simple way of construing ignorance as it appears in *The Ignorant Schoolmaster* is to follow Rancière in his description of emancipatory teachers as those who 'could teach what they themselves were ignorant of' (Rancière, this volume, p. 1). That is to say, the emancipatory school-master teaches things that he doesn't know about. In this sense, ignorance stands for some type of void. Ignorance consists of that which is not known, and not grasped. Indeed, this first sort of ignorance accounts for how *The Ignorant Schoolmaster* has been generally received. At first glance, it seems that Rancière is referring to an emancipatory pedagogy that can hold tight to the void of ignorance. Actually, though, this understanding of Rancière's text is problematic. It is problematic if one looks closely at Jacotot's foundational experience of emancipatory pedagogy. It is problematic precisely because Jacotot's Flemish speaking students, although they spoke a language Jacotot knew nothing of, were actually learning a language Jacotot knew *everything* about. Jacotot was hardly ignorant of the French his students were learning. So in this foundational experience, he was only half ignorant. He was ignorant of where his students were coming from, but he was knowledgeable about where they were going.

1/2 ignorant

Ignorance connotes more than a void in Rancière's work. It connotes as well the very agnostic relation to truth that we have been describing. This is the ignorance we have examined earlier, an 'ignorance which liberates' (Rancière 2006a, p. 3). Jacotot is ignorant of Flemish, this is true. But that is only half of his ignorance. The other half has to do with an ignorance about any 'discourse that separates truth from illusion' (Rancière 2006a. p. 10). It is an insistence on a certain agnosticism regarding any 'truth' as to how his students got from the state of not knowing French, to the state of knowing French. There is simply no way for Jacotot to adjudicate one discourse, that of French, by means of another, that of Flemish. Instead he insists on ignoring any supposed truth about the ways these two discourses might be bound together. These two discourses are not bound by any adjudicating knowledge. They are bound only by the will of the student and the will of the instructor. The emancipatory pedagogue may practice a passive form of ignorance, it is true. He or she may choose to remain void of particular knowledges. But the emancipatory pedagogue will also practice a more general, active form of ignorance: an ignoring of truth.

As we have shown in this chapter, Rancière's agnostic perspective on truth is key both to his criticism of the school's explanatory regime and to his new logic of emancipation. This perspective on truth should come as no surprise since Rancière describes his own work as that of a storyteller, or a polemicist. Yet, this perspective on truth is one that does not settle easily within the common intellectual discourses of today, discourses that usually aim to *get at* truth rather than to proceed *in spite of* truth. And so one finds that even the work of a storyteller or polemicist is easily dissected in terms of its truth, its essence, its relation to other truths. It is against this tendency to get at some fundamental truth in Rancière's work that we situated the preceding chapter. We demonstrated that the truth of Rancière's work could not be found in terms of the social struggle for recognition. Now we will look again to the realm of words, which, as we have seen, 'fragment' truth rather than offering some royal road to truth. In particular, we look to words in the mouths of those who learn.

CHAPTER 7

LEARNER, STUDENT, SPEAKER

A learner is not a shedhand or barrower, but a budding shearer who has not yet shorn 5,000 sheep (10,000 in Queensland).

(Gunn 1965, p. 35)

INTRODUCTION

In this chapter, we return to the question of speech. We do this by asking a simple question: How shall we call those whom we teach and who, in a manner of speaking, are the subjects of education? We ask this question because we believe that language matters. This is not because language has some kind of mysterious power, but more simply because words are connected to other words, so that using one particular word leads more easily to some words than to others. We are not, therefore, aiming at unearthing underlying assumptions – as this would suggest a fundamental distinction between surface and depth – but of following pathways of meaning and expression. Such pathways enact a particular distribution of the sensible and in this way articulate particular relations between ways of saying, ways of doing and ways of being. And, that is why our words matter.

LEARNER

The English language has several words to refer to those who are the subjects of education. Some of those words map rather neatly onto similar words in other languages, although other languages also have words that cannot so easily be translated into English.[1] Here, we are particularly interested in one of the words used to designate those who are the subjects of education, which is the word 'learner'. If our analysis is correct – and there is empirical support for our thesis (see Haugsbakk and Nordkvelle 2007) – the word 'learner' has over the past two or three decades rapidly gained prominence in the English-speaking world. We can see this in policy documents, in educational research and in everyday speech about education (see Biesta 2004; 2009). The rise of the word 'learner' is part of the emergence of the rise of a 'new language of learning' – a language which refers to students as learners, to teachers as facilitators of learning, to schools as places for learning, to vocational education as the learning and skills sector, to grown ups as adult learners and so on. The ambition articulated in the language of learning can partly be understood as an emancipatory one, albeit through an 'old logic' of emancipation, in that it can be interpreted as an attempt to shift the emphasis away from teachers, curricula, schools and other 'input factors' to the activities and identities of those who are supposed to benefit from this. The rise of the language of learning and of the designation of students as learners can thus, in a sense, be seen as an attempt to liberate the learner – first and foremost from the teacher but also from the wider educational system. But this gain is also a loss. Why is that so?

We can start from the simple observation that in order to call someone a learner there must be something for this person to learn. This 'something' can be almost anything: knowledge, values, under-standings, skills, dispositions, capacities, competencies, criticality, identity, autonomy and so on – as long as it can be learned. What is striking about calling someone a learner is, however, not what it is that needs to be learned; what matters is the fact that the learner is constructed in terms of a *lack*. The learner is the one who is missing something. The learner is the one who is not yet complete. Perhaps after shearing ten sheep one may well feel competent as a sheep shearer, but it takes another 4,990 sheep – and in Queensland even 9,900 sheep – before one loses the identity of a learner. In the United Kingdom, the learner identity is very visible when one is a 'learner-driver', as this requires that one attaches learner plates to one's car – a big 'L' at the front and a big 'L' at the back – until one has gained formal authorization to drive a motor vehicle. Calling students 'learners' or referring to grown ups as 'adult learners' is not fundamentally different from this. It basically means that we attach learning plates to them in order to indicate that they are *not yet*: not yet knowledgeable, not yet skilful, not yet competent, not yet autonomous and so on. It is difficult to see this as just a case of liberation.

To call someone a learner thus suggests an inequality between those who have learned, those who know, can, or are, and those who still need to learn in order to know, be able, or be. This, in itself, is not a problem. If one wishes to shear sheep or drive a car, there are indeed things that must be learned and skills that must be mastered. Once this has been done successfully we can consider ourselves equal to those who already know and can. Problems arise when it is claimed that the trajectory from ignorance to knowledge, or from inability to ability, *necessarily* requires the intervention of an educator on the assumption that learners are not yet capable to learn by themselves. Whereas there is, therefore, a weak construction of the learner as the one who needs to learn something he does not yet know or is able to do, there is also a strong construction of the learner as the one who is not able to learn for herself, that is, *without* the intervention of an educator. This strong construction of the learner suggests a more fundamental lack. Here, the learner is not simply lacking what it is that needs to be learned; here the learner is lacking the very *capacity* to learn without the intervention of the educator. The arguments for this idea are well known to educators. They are basically of two kinds: developmental and curricular. The developmental argument says that the child has not yet developed sufficiently in order to be able to learn this particular thing. It says, for example, that the child's intelligence has not yet sufficiently matured or that we are waiting for the frontal lobes to catch up. The curricular argument says that the subject matter is too difficult to be understood as it is; it therefore needs to be broken down by the teacher into smaller bits, and then sequenced in such a way that, step by step, the learner will be able to reach understanding. Thus, we put learners onto educational respirators for the time being – that is, until they can breath for themselves. Until that moment, the main task of the teacher is to explain to the learner what the learner cannot yet understand for herself.

Explanation thus offers itself 'as a means to reduce the situation of inequality where those who know nothing are in relation with those who know' (Rancière, this volume, p. 3). But, does it? Explanation may well give the impression that it does. Many will have experienced a situation in which something was explained to them and, upon hearing this, they said 'I see'. But, it was not that the explicator could see this for them and just handed it over – they still had to see it for themselves. Perhaps then what is communicated through the act of explanation is not the explanation itself – in order to understand, the learner still has to figure out for himself what is being explained to him – but the idea that explanation is *indispensable*, that is, that the learner is unable to understand *without* explanation. This is the point Rancière makes when he suggests that 'to explain something to someone is first of all to show him he cannot understand it by himself' (Rancière 1991a, p. 6). To explain, in other words, 'is to demonstrate an incapacity' (Rancière, this volume, p. 3).

Rather than bridging the gap between the one who does not know and the one who knows, rather than transforming inequality into equality, explanation actually enacts and in a sense inaugurates and then perpetually confirms this inequality. It is not so much, therefore, that a learner is the one who needs explanation; it is rather that the act of explanation constitutes the learner as the one who is unable to learn *without* explanation, *without* the intervention of a 'master-explicator'. The learner is, in other words, the *product* of the 'explicative order' (Rancière 1991a, p. 4), not the one who makes the explicative order necessary. This is how, as we have seen, the explicative order is founded upon the 'myth of pedagogy', which is 'the parable of a world divided into knowing minds and ignorant ones, the capable and the incapable, the intelligent and the stupid' (Rancière 1991a, p. 6). It is why the explicator's 'special trick' consists of a 'double inaugural gesture' (ibid., p. 6).

> On the one hand, he decrees the absolute beginning: it is only now that the act of learning will begin. On the other, having thrown a veil of ignorance over everything that is to be learned, he appoints himself to the task of lifting it'. (ibid., pp. 6–7)

The intention behind this is generally a laudable one, as the teacher aims 'to transmit his knowledge to his students so as to bring them, by degrees, to his own level of expertise' (ibid., p. 3). The 'art' of the schoolmaster, 'who methodically lifts the veil from that which the student could not understand alone, is the art that promises the student will one day be the equal of the schoolmaster' (Rancière, this volume, p. 5). But, will this promise ever be delivered? Is it ever possible to escape from the circle of explanation? Or, is it the case that as soon as one starts out on a trajectory of explanation, one will be there forever, always trying to catch up, always trying to understand what the explicator already understands, but always in need of the explicator's explanation in order to understand? Viewed in this way explanation 'is something completely different from a practical means of reaching some end' but rather appears to be an end in itself. Explanation is 'the infinite verification of a fundamental axiom: the axiom of inequality' (Rancière, this volume, p. 3). Is it the case, therefore, that as soon as one becomes a learner one has automatically become a *lifelong* learner?

STUDENT

Is it possible to break away from the circle of powerlessness 'that ties the student to the explicator' (Rancière 1991a, p. 15)? It is possible to engage in education in such a way that it emancipates rather than stultifies? Perhaps. But the way to do this is not through the introduction of more 'refined' or more 'progressive' forms of explanation.

> The distinction between 'stultification' and 'emancipation' is not a distinction between methods of instruction. It is not a distinction between traditional or authoritarian methods, on the one hand, and new or active methods, on the other: stultification can and does happen in all kinds of active and modern ways. (Rancière, this volume, p. 6)

Is it possible, therefore, to teach without explanation? As we have seen, Rancière makes a case that this is possible and, more importantly, that it is only when we engage in teaching without explanation that it may be possible to emancipate rather than stultify.

Illustrating this possibility, Rancière describes the relationship between Jacotot and his students not as a relationship of intelligence to intelligence but of 'will to will' (Rancière 1991a, p. 13). Whereas stultification takes place 'whenever one intelligence is subordinated to another', emancipation takes place when an intelligence obeys only itself 'even while the will obeys another will' (ibid., p. 13). What is at the heart of emancipatory education, therefore, is the act of revealing 'an intelligence to itself' (ibid., p. 28). And what this requires from the student is attention, that is, 'absolute attention for seeing and seeing again, saying and repeating' (ibid., p. 23). The route that students will take when summoned to use their intelligence is, as we have discussed previously, entirely unknown, but what the student cannot escape, Rancière argues, is 'the exercise of his liberty' and this is summoned by a three-part question 'What do you see? What do you think about it? What do you make of it? And so on, to infinity' (ibid., p. 23). This is why there are therefore only two 'fundamental acts' for the master: 'He *interrogates*, he demands speech, that is to say, the manifestation of an intelligence that wasn't aware of itself or that had given up' and 'he *verifies* that the work of the intelligence is done with attention' (ibid., p. 29; emphasis in original). What is verified is not the *outcome* of the use of intelligence, as this would return the process to that of explanation, but only the *use* of intelligence, that is, that the work of the intelligence is done with attention.

As we have pointed out, this interrogation should not be understood in the Socratic way where the sole purpose of interrogation is to lead the student to a point that is already known by the master. While this 'may be the path to learning', it is 'in no way a path to emancipation' (ibid., p. 29) because central to emancipation is the consciousness 'of what an intelligence can do when it considers itself equal to any other and considers any other equal to itself' (ibid., p. 39). Thus, what constantly needs to be verified is 'the principle of the equality of all speaking beings' (ibid., p. 39), the belief that 'there is no hierarchy of *intellectual capacity*' but only 'inequality in the *manifestations* of intelligence' (ibid., p. 27). After all, 'what stultifies the common people is not the lack of instruction, but the belief in the inferiority of their intelligence' (ibid., p. 39). 'The emancipatory teacher's call forbids the supposed ignorant one the satisfaction of what is known, the satisfaction of admitting that one is incapable of knowing more' (Rancière, this volume, p. 6). The only thing that is needed, therefore, is to remind people that they can see and think for themselves and are not dependent upon others who claim that they can see and think for them.

Jacotot's approach is therefore not anti-authoritarian. It is not an approach that tries to liberate the learner by de-authorizing the educator so that education dissolves into learning – either individual learning or collective learning. The educator is still there, but not as an explicator, not as a superior intelligence, but as a will, as someone who demands the effort from the student and verifies that an effort has been made. 'The ignorant person will learn by himself what the master doesn't know if the master believes he can and obliges him to realize his capacity' (Rancière 1991a, p. 15). This at once changes the identity of the one who is the subject of education. It is no longer that of a learner; it is no longer that of someone whose intelligence is subordinated to another and therefore needs explanation in order to be 'lifted up' to the level of the explicator.[2] The one who is the subject of education is summoned to *study* and thus, in the most literal sense, has become a *student*.

SPEAKER

It is tempting to read Rancière's pedagogical ideas in psychological terms and understand them as a theory of teaching and learning. From that angle, there are, on the one hand, some startling claims that seem to fly in the face of what we know, for example, about child development or about curriculum and instruction. On the other hand, there are some more familiar ideas that seem to resonate with constructivist views about how people learn. But Rancière's point is actually not about 'a better pedagogy' but about an entirely different route, 'that of liberty' (Rancière 1991a, p. 14) and emancipation. Rancière's point is a political one and *therefore* a thoroughly educational point – that is, if we see education as being concerned with emancipation and freedom (see Biesta 2006). And the question that is at stake in all this is a very simple one: Who can speak?

Again, this question should not be read in psychological terms. The question here is not about who has the ability or capacity to speak – which would at the same time suggest that there are some who are disabled or incapacitated in the domain of speech. The question who can speak is, in a sense, about who is *allowed* to speak. But the 'in a sense' is important here, as we shouldn't read 'being allowed' in terms of the master who claims the power to decide whether his learners are allowed to open their mouths or not. Such a reading would locate the question as to who can speak within the framework of a philosophy of recognition (Honneth 1996) that starts from the assumption of inequality – where some claim the power to let others speak and where some see themselves in need of permission by powerful others before they feel they can speak – and hence is still reproducing the very inequality and exclusion it seeks to overcome. This is another way, then, of depicting what happens under the 'explicative order', as one can see explanation as the attempt to bring those who are considered as not yet able to speak to a level of reason and understanding where they can begin to speak in a way that is considered to 'make sense'. Viewing things in this way not only suggests that learners start out by making 'noise' rather than producing 'voice'. It also implies that they need a master to explain to them what their noise actually means. To gain voice in this way would mean that the master needs to tell the learners what they are thinking and saying – which at the very same time 'overwrites' their own thought and speech and thus denies them their 'capacity' for thought and speech. To say that the question as to who can speak is about who is allowed to speak, is therefore not about trying to point at someone who has the power to let others speak, but refers to a particular distribution of the sensible in which some 'sound' exists as 'noise' and other 'sound' exists as 'voice'.

One can speak within a particular distribution of the sensible. In that case, speaking is a matter of identification, of taking up an existing identity, an existing place within the existing order. But this is not the only way in which one can 'come into speech' (see also Hallward 2005). Instead of being an act of identification, speaking can also be an act of subjectification. That is, speaking need not be about taking up an identity that is already waiting for us. If our speaking is supplementary to the existing distribution of the sensible, if our speaking introduces an element that is heterogeneous to this distribution, then our speaking can 'test' the equality of any and every speaking being. The distinction between the two ways in which we can speak is perhaps less sharp than it may look. At one level, it is only the latter kind of speech – speaking as subjectification – that seems to have the power to 'decompose and recompose' a particular distribution of the sensible and that, in this sense, can count as speech with political 'effects' in the sense in which Rancière defines politics. It is the kind of speech that produces 'new inscriptions of equality' within the police order (Rancière 1999, p. 42).

But the 'force' of such inscriptions of equality is not only a matter of quality but also of quantity. Speech as subjectification also produces new and different opportunities for identification – it produces, as Rancière puts it, 'a fresh sphere of visibility for further demonstrations' (ibid.; emphasis added) – and such identifications add to what we might call the 'force' or 'weight' of the initial political 'act'. Speaking as identification is therefore not necessarily without political significance. What matters is whether the identification is with 'inscriptions of equality' within the police order or not. The idea of 'inscriptions of equality' therefore also indicates that we should not think of the distinction between the police order and politics in moral terms, that is, as 'bad' versus 'good' or as 'not having to do with equality' and 'having to do with equality'. We have seen that

Rancière (1999, pp. 30–31) emphasizes that 'there is a worse and a better police' – which is why institutions matter and why speech as identification can have political significance too. The better police is, however, not the one 'that adheres to the supposedly natural order of society or the science of legislators', but the one 'that all the breaking and entering perpetrated by egalitarian logic has most jolted out of its "natural" logic' (ibid., p. 31). Thus, the police order 'can produce all sorts of good, and one kind of police may be infinitely preferable to another' (ibid.). But as we have seen, whether police is 'sweet and kind' (ibid.) does not make it any less the opposite of politics.

When we refer to those who are the subjects of education as 'learners' we immediately put them in a position where they still have to learn and where their learning is considered to be dependent upon our explanation. Hence, we are saying that they cannot yet speak. We are saying that, for the moment, until the 'end' of education has arrived, they can only produce noise and that it is only as a result of our explanation of the meaning of their noise that they can come to speech – which, as we have argued above, means that they will never be able to come to their *own* speech. When we refer to those who are the subjects of education as 'students', we start from the assumption that they can learn *without* our explanations, without the need for an educational 'respirator'. In this sense, we enact – and perhaps we could add: inaugurate – a different relationship: one of will to will, not of intelligence to intelligence. In doing so, we are denying that our students should acquire a new, additional intelligence – that of the master's explications (see Rancière 1991a, p. 8) – and it is this that is implied in Rancière's insistence that emancipatory education starts from the assumption of the equality of intelligence of all human beings. This does not mean 'that all the actions of all intelligences are the same', but rather highlights 'that there is only one intelligence at work in all intellectual training' (Rancière, this volume, p. 5). Emancipatory schoolmasters do nothing more (but also nothing less) than demanding that their students make use of their intelligence. They forbid 'the supposed ignorant one the satisfaction (. . .) of admitting that one is incapable of knowing more' (ibid.). But just to say that our students should study is not yet enough. There is, after all, a critical distinction to be made between those who become students of the explications of others – and the world is full of such explications – and those who follow their own 'orbits' (Rancière 1991a, p. 59). What matters, therefore, is not so much that students study but that they *speak*. As Rancière suggests, our intelligence's 'leading virtue [is] the poetic virtue' (ibid., p. 64). In the act of speaking, man doesn't transmit his knowledge, he makes poetry; he translates and invites others to do the same' (ibid., p. 65). And precisely here lies the significance of Rancière's observation that the emancipatory schoolmaster 'demands *speech*, that is to say, the manifestation of an intelligence that wasn't aware of itself or that had given up' (ibid., p. 29; emphasis added).

ME TOO, I'M A SPEAKER

Emancipatory education can therefore be characterized as education that starts from the assumption that all students can speak – or to be more precise: that all students can *already* speak. It starts from the assumption that students neither lack a capacity for speech, nor that they are producing noise. It starts from the assumption, in other words, that students already are *speakers*. This is not, of course, how the advocates of the explicative order would see it. 'They suppose a little animal who, bumping into things, explores a world that he isn't yet able to see and will only discern when they teach him to do so' (Rancière 1991a, p. 11). The emancipatory schoolmaster, on the other hand, starts from the assumption that 'the human child is first of all a speaking being' (ibid.).

> The child who repeats the words he hears and the Flemish student 'lost' in his *Télémaque* are not proceeding hit or miss. All their effort, all their exploration, is strained toward this: someone has addressed words to them that they want to recognize and respond to, not as students or as learned men, but as people; in the way you respond to someone speaking to you and not to someone examining you: under the sign of equality. (ibid.)

Surely, the sounds newborns make are quite alien to our ears. But when we classify such sounds as noise, we are not stating a psychological fact but are introducing a political distinction. We are saying that they lack the capacity to speak and are thereby suggesting that they need to be told what their sounds mean – which also means that we put ourselves in the position to be able to tell them this. When we do so, we start from the assumption of inequality and are thus caught in the circle of powerlessness. The alternative is not to try to compensate for or bridge inequality, but simply to start from some-where else, that is from the assumption of the equality of all speaking beings. After all, 'Equality is not given, nor is it claimed; it is practiced, it is *verified*' (Rancière 1999, p. 137). But, it can only appear 'as a tautology or an absurdity' (Rancière 1991a, p. 15) because it introduces an element that is heterogeneous to the circle of power-lessness. To start from the assumption that students *are* speakers is, therefore, 'the most difficult leap' (ibid., p. 16), but 'one must dare to recognize it and pursue the *open* verification of its power' (ibid.; emphasis in original).

To start from the assumption of the equality of all speaking beings is not to assume, naively, that equality *exists*. It is not to assume, naively, that one has a special insight into how inequality exists and how it can be transformed into equality. 'About inequality', Rancière writes, 'There is nothing to know' (Rancière 1991a, p. 46).

> Inequality is no more a given to be transformed by knowledge than equality is an end to be transmitted through knowledge. Equality and inequality are not two states. They are two 'opinions', that is to say two distinct axioms, by which educational training can operate, two axioms that have nothing in common. All that one can do is verify the axiom one is given. The schoolmaster's explanatory logic presents inequality axiomatically. . . . The ignor-ant schoolmaster's logic poses equality as an axiom to be verified. It relates the state of inequality in the teacher-student relation not to the promise of an equality-to-come that will never come, but to the reality of a basic equality. In order for the ignorant one to do the exercises commanded by the master, the ignorant one must already understand what the master says. There is an equality of speaking beings that comes before the relation of inequality, one that sets the stage for inequality's very existence. (Rancière, this volume, pp. 4–5)

The point, in short, is not to prove the equality of intelligence. 'It's seeing what can be done under that supposition' (Rancière 1991a, p. 46), under that 'beautiful lie' (Rancière 2006a, p. 10).

We have already mentioned that the 'explicative order' is not just an educational logic. It is at the very same time, and perhaps first and foremost, a *social* logic and the name of this logic is 'progress'. 'Progress is the pedagogical fiction built into the fiction of society as a whole. At the heart of the pedagogical fiction is the representation of inequality as a *retard* in one's development' (Rancière 1991a, p. 118). That is why progress needs public instruction as its 'secular arm' (ibid., p. 131). But as soon as one sets out on the path of progress, as soon as one sets out 'to make an equal society out of unequal men', one has only one way to go, which is 'the integral pedagogicization of society – the general infantilization of the individuals that make it up' (ibid., p. 133). 'Later', Rancière adds, 'this will be called continuing education, that is to say, the coextension of the explicatory institution with society' (ibid.). It is in relation to this that Rancière singles out Joseph Jacotot as being alone 'in recognizing the effacement of equality under progress, of emancipation under instruction" and as being the only one who "refused all progressive and pedagogical translation of emancipatory equality' (ibid., p. 134). It is against this background that Rancière warns that emancipation cannot be mediated by social institutions. The 'heavy price to pay' for the insight that 'there are no stages to equality' – since as soon as we begin to think of equality as something that can be achieved starting from inequality we have already given up the possibility of equality – is that 'there is no social emancipation, and no emancipatory school'. (Rancière, this volume, p. 9) The reason for this stems from the insight that 'explanation is a social method, the method by which inequality gets represented and reproduced, and if the institution is the place where this representation operates, it follows that intellectual emancipation is necessarily distinct from social and institutional logic' (ibid.). Although it does therefore matter how we refer to those who are the subjects of education, it matters – and perhaps we could say: it matters only – as a verification of the axiom of equality. It is not a strategy that can be explained and can then be implemented to make schools more progressive or emancipatory. The explicative order can, in other words, not be replaced by an emancipatory order. The circle of powerlessness can only be interrupted by starting from somewhere else, by starting from a different assumption – the assumption of equality – in order to see what can be done under that supposition. The suggestion to refer to students as speakers provides such a starting point – not a conclusion.

CHAPTER 8

CONCLUSION: THE WORLD IS NOT A SCHOOL

In 1994, a short, disparaging review of Rancière's *The Ignorant Schoolmaster* appeared in the journal *French Studies*, a review offered here in full not because we wish to advertise its message, but rather on account of the way it underscores the insidiousness of a society pedagogicized.

This book, first published in French in 1987, consists of a meditation on the significance of the radical pedagogy of Joseph Jacotot, a late eighteenth-century schoolteacher turned soldier who settled in the Kingdom of Belgium-Holland with the return of the Bourbons. Meditation is the right word, for the author, a well-known left-wing intellectual, originally close to Althusser, does not so much offer an account of Jacotot's ideas and their influence as use them as a platform to expound the road to true liberation in a post-Marxist world. Indeed, it is often difficult to tell from the text where Jacotot ends and Rancière begins. Rancière believes Jacotot's insight is of profound importance for the present: it contains the liberating message that we all can and should belong to the chattering classes. Individual liberation stems from a change of will, not a change in society. It is not the place of a historian of French ancien-regime education to comment on the plausibility of Rancière's educational philosophy, nor is it the reviewer's place, given the way that the book is written, to bemoan the lack of detailed information about Jacotot's educational beliefs and practice. Suffice it to say that both subject and author evidently owe much to the Rousseauist and in some ways conservative strand of the Enlightenment which stressed that a change in society without a change in man was pointless. Equally, there is an obvious existentialist streak in Rancière. Whether there was a need for this translation is another matter. As the interesting introduction by

Kristin Ross makes clear, the text can be best understood in the light of the arguments within the French socialist party in the 1980s over educational reform, and in the broader perspective of the Left's conviction that bourgeois society was here to stay. It is a work, then, firmly cemented in a specific Parisian context, which is already somewhat outdated with the return to power of the Right. Outside France, and in the Anglo-Saxon world especially, the work is unlikely to find a large audience. In an age of growing unemployment across the continent, working men and women are unlikely to gain much comfort from the thought that enforced leisure will give them the opportunity to channel their energies into creative discourse. Europe's autodidacts seem destined, as ever, to be a small minority, left to communicate with themselves and nature, like Rousseau on the Ile de Saint-Pierre. (1994, pp. 104–105)

What are we to do with the writing of Rancière? Where are we to put it? How are we to characterize it, and to which discipline, or disciplines, are we to assign it? If we follow the logic of this short review, we will know, as this reviewer does, a few things about the inadequacies of Rancière's work. We will know first of all that Rancière's writings are infected by his status as a left-wing intellectual. We will know that to expect a balanced presentation of Jacotot's pedagogy by Rancière will be to expect the impossible as a result of his former proximity to Louis Althusser, this in spite of his break with Althusser. Too, we will be aware that because Rancière does not offer enough specific details about Jacotot's teaching practices, he is not an accurate historian. We will know that his educational thought owes a great deal to Rousseau and the insistence on individual, rather than social, transformation. And, of course, that his thought serves a debt to 1980s French arguments over educational reform. This fact, in turn, shows that Rancière's *Schoolmaster* will already have been out of date since the world has moved on. We are already in the third millennium, looking back not only on the 1980s but also on the 1990s. Furthermore, we will be convinced, if we believe this review, that Rancière's work will get no reception in the English-speaking world. And finally, we will know that this text is fundamentally an argument for the lonely practice of auto-didacticism, a practice that implicitly characterizes Rancière's own work, offering another reason why his work will itself remain lonely.

While it is possible to argue against these matters, point by point, and thus to explain why this review is wrong, such an explanation is absolutely incommensurable with the intervention on Rancière's work that we have proposed in this book. In fact, if we were to explain the awkwardness of what we learn from this review, we would paradoxically be shoring up its claims. For what we learn from this review resides on two levels. On one level, we learn the 'facts' above. They are dubious facts but they are authorized by the pen of the reviewer and by the status of the journal in which the review appears. They are presented as a set of conclusions. This review concludes certain things about Rancière's writing. On another level, though, this review uses its conclusions to *explain* certain things about Rancière and his work. In this review, it is explained that Rancière is a certain type of intellectual, a certain quality of historian, that he is influenced by a certain tradition in educational philosophy, that he is the product of a certain decade, and, finally, it is explained that there is a certain lonely quality to his intellectualism. In short, this review has taken Rancière to school. It explains where he stands in the subject areas of history and philosophy. It explains how his friends and family affect the quality of his schoolwork. It explains what school class he graduated with – the class of the 1980s. And, it explains what kind of a learner he is – lonely.

To argue against this set of explanations is to join in the act of explaining. It is to send Rancière back to school if only to argue that he is *better* in history and philosophy than his report card indicates, that his friends *don't* interfere with his schoolwork, that he is *not* stuck in the 1980s and that he *does* learn well with others. To argue with this review would entail showing how the teacher is not knowledgeable enough. By the teacher's own admission, he is 'ignorant' of educational philosophy and educational practice. To argue with this teacher would require saying that one knows more than he about these matters. To argue in such a way is precisely to enact the explanatory order that we wish not to enact. It means schooling Rancière rather than intervening on his work. Instead of arguing with this review, let it stand as an example of what *not* to do with Rancière's work. How easy it is, in a society pedagogicized, to do the easiest thing of all – to explain the speech of another.

In scholarly writing, especially, it is particularly tempting to speak in a way that is policing rather than in a way that changes the redistribution of the sensible. It is tempting to speak not in the manner of

a child, but in the manner of an adult. The scholar is an adult who
has gone to school. Because of this attendance, this adult knows
how to school others with his or her thought. The adult knows how
to explain. The adult knows how to arrive at truth. As a child, on
the other hand, one is ignorant of truth. One does not yet know the
practices of an explanatory order. One does not yet know how to
follow, in an orderly way, the thoughts of others. One does not know
how to queue up. One moves instead from proximity to proximity.
One does not yet know that the world is not meant to be a school.
Instead of taking Jacques Rancière to school, one should proceed as
a child who looks forwards to the sound of a bell. One should speak
as if truant.

THE WORLD IS NOT EXPLAINED BY THE SCHOOL

In one respect it is, of course, obvious that the world is not a school.
Schools, for one thing, are buildings in which schooling is practised
by teachers and students who encounter each other in their role
as teachers and students. The world, on the other hand, is everywhere
and allows for a multitude of roles, identities and encounters. In
this respect, schools are not only confined *spaces*, they also entail
confined *practices*, practices with limits and boundaries. Perhaps one
of the most prominent limits that is set and enacted by schools is a
limit on interpretation. To the extent to which schools are set up
as institutions for the transmission of knowledge, skills and values,
they are not simply there to transmit but also to *sanction* certain
knowledge, skills and values as valuable, as correct, or even as true.
Schools not only do this at the input side of the process, for example
through the construction of curricula that specify what ought to be
learned and the development of pedagogies that are aimed to get
the right message across. Since all teachers know that what teachers
teach is not necessarily the same as what students learn, they also
work on the output side, most notably through assessment: reward-
ing those students who come up with the right interpretations and
identifying those who have not yet managed as being in need of more
education – until they get it right.

To say that Rancière's work helps us see that the world is not a
school is not done in order to be able to highlight the differences
between schools and the world – they are, as we said, obvious. To say
that the world is not a school is rather to say that the world *ought not*

to be like a school, and reading the statement in this way actually begins to make it possible to see the ways in which, and the extent to which, societies do actually operate like schools and also to see why and how that is problematic. While one can characterize schools as institutions that set a limit on interpretation, this does not mean, therefore, that there are no such limits in society. There is not only a lot of active policing of interpretations going on in society – and those who are involved in the explicit policing of interpretations will often try to argue that they are doing this for good reasons and sometimes these reasons are indeed good. In Rancière's vocabulary we could say that the sensible *has* to be distributed in some way – it cannot *not* be distributed – and that society cannot be completely 'out of order.' The 'choice,' therefore, is not between *arche* and *an-arche* but between 'worse' and 'better' police. And all the quotation marks are important here, first of all because the 'choice' is not a choice that can be made from some neutral place, with all options open and on the table, so to speak. The choice is much more an experimental one: jolting a particular distribution of the sensible without much guarantee about what will happen next. However, not any jolt will do. The distinction between 'worse' and 'better' police is a distinction – and perhaps also a judgment – that must take *equality* as its reference point. This is why emancipation is not simply about disrupting any limits set on interpretation. It is not simply about giving free reign to the truth. And this is also why total freedom of interpretation – if it is appropriate to use the word 'freedom' in this context – is not the same as equality.

The arbitrariness of language is therefore not in itself political or emancipatory. Everything depends on whether one's speaking and acting starts from the assumption of equality and is aimed at its verification, or whether it starts from the assumption of inequality. Explanation is a way of speaking, being, and doing that enacts the latter assumption. While again we might start from locating the practice of explanation firmly and safely in the school and assume a different set of social relationships operating in society, Rancière's work helps us to see the extent to which explanation also operates in society – as a social logic – thus modelling social and policing relations according to an explicative notion of schooling. The explicative order represents inequality in *temporal* terms, that is, as a retard in one's development, and thus presents time as the great emancipator. The explicative order always comes with a promise: the promise that things will be different in the future, that after graduation, when one has caught up, equality will arrive. That will be the moment when the third world will have become equal to the first world (probably mopping up the second world along the way); it will be the moment where there is no longer a need for lifelong learning and where no child has been left behind. The promise entailed in the explicative order also comes with an assignment – with homework, so to speak. It involves assessment by those who have identified the ones who still need to catch up, thus putting those who do the identifying in a position to judge whether the homework has already been done well enough. The eschatological gesture of the explicative order not only raises the question whether it is ever possible to catch up once one has been identified as lagging behind; the question is also whether catching up is where one would want to go in the first place. If we are serious about equality, we therefore need to steer away from the explicative order, from turning the world into a school in which some set the terms for the remediation of others; we should steer away, in other words, from using explanation as an excuse for not taking equality seriously.

JACQUES RANCIÈRE IS NOT A SCHOOL

In might seem obvious to say that a person is not a school. However, there is a sense in which Jacques Rancière might become a school. One can see this in the way that Rancière's work has fostered a wave of scholarship and intellectual activity. Rancière's work is seconded by schools of recognition, by art schools, by schools of philosophy. It is touted in conferences, on blogspots, in books such as this one. And the schooling of Rancière is becoming rife among those who look to his work on pedagogy. For, it is easy to discern a pedagogical method to follow in *The Ignorant Schoolmaster*; this, in spite of the protests of Jacotot himself. The reader of *The Ignorant Schoolmaster* can easily take the position of Jacotot's own followers who, in spite of Jacotot's protests, attempted to spread the gospel of Jacotot's style in an effort to foster the general growth of intellectual emancipation. Jacotot himself denied that his version of emancipatory equality could be translated into some educational program for progress. Nevertheless, there remains a clear jacotist method to be found. Rancière, like Jacotot, tries to abolish this method. He does so with his own dramatization of the fall of Jacotot's universal teaching.

The denouement of *The Ignorant Schoolmaster* is, after all, the failure of Jacotot's method. As Rancière posits, universal teaching will never take, but also that it may never perish. The act of universal education is the only way for people to follow their own intellectual paths. Nonetheless, universal education will never take as a method to be duplicated. Indeed, any close reading of *The Ignorant Schoolmaster* yields that the *fall* of Jacotot is more significant than any possible success of his method. This fall narrates the demise of any educational method that goes to school. Jacotot's method could not stand the test of time precisely because others took it as explanatory.

Add to this demise one's experience of the book itself. One reads *The Ignorant Schoolmaster*. One is the reader of an educational method that claims not to be a method. And as one reads this book, there is the distinct feeling that whatever is claimed or disavowed by either Jacotot or Rancière is claimed or disavowed by some admixture of the two. As Rancière's voice narrates Jacotot, then quotes Jacotot, then slips largely into being the same voice as Jacotot, it is not at all clear whom we are reading. Is it Rancière? Is it Jacotot? Stylistically, then, Rancière turns jacotist method into an admixture of two methods – his and Jacotot's. If Jacotot's method does not survive, it is difficult to know who, precisely, let it die out. Was it Jacotot who gave up on his own method, or is it Rancière who has let the method die, once again, two centuries later.

Even more interesting are the teachings of this book that claims not to teach. If we are sympathetic to Jacotot's (or Rancière's) teachings, we have in front of us a book, an educational path, to follow, but the path has been shown to be un-followable through Rancière's staging, through the path's end. We are thus sympathetic not to Jacotot's educational method, but to its story, nor to Rancière's educational method, but to *its* story. The book leaves us with a method that can only be a story, and this book is educative precisely in the sense that it forces its reader to translate its contents into his or her experience without any certainty as to how its contents are to be translated. That is to say, the book is to be read without a teaching. This book is, as Rancière will put it elsewhere, akin to the idiom of the artist, as well as the researcher. The book provides a story that calls for readers who will render their own translation. It calls for those who read it to become emancipated storytellers in their own right. Faced with a book whose effect cannot be anticipated because its method cannot be generalized, one is left to one's own experience of the book's words. One is taught, but only in story.

It is against this backdrop of Rancière's *story* that we find it necessary to warn against schooling Rancière. There are a number of ways that one might decide to implement Rancière's educational work, any of which would be missing the central point to Rancière's educational story, namely, that it is a story rather than a method. In order *not* to school Rancière, it is important to de-link his thinking from other prevalent educational traditions in the following ways. First, Rancière is not another progressive educator whose work radicalizes the experiential aspects of progressivism. His is not a recipe for educational success predicated on the most intimate contact between student and curriculum. This, despite the fact that Jacotot's students were in unmediated contact with their curriculum, the *Télémaque*. Second, Rancière's is not a method of radicalized constructivism. It is the case that a central tenet of constructivism is that the learner must initiate progress from where he or she resides intellectually, rather than accepting the lectured imposition of the instructor's knowledge. However, Rancière's work is not a recipe for the abdication of lectureship. Third, Rancière, as we have stressed repeatedly, is not a recent iteration of critical pedagogy. Indeed, we have focused on emancipation. However, we have also stressed that emancipation may or may not turn out to be an educational concern. One could continue this list of what Rancière's educational work is *not* a recipe for. The point here is quite simply that Rancière's educational work is not a recipe for *any* kind of pedagogy. It is a story. It is not a method. It waits not for implementation. It waits instead for another story to be told in return.

BUT THE WORLD STILL HAS SCHOOLS

While we may have established, then, that the world is not a school and also why it is generally not a good idea to model the world as a school, we still have a world full of schools. So, what should we do with them? Should we read Rancière's work as a critique of the very institution of the school and the very idea of schooling? Is it an argument for the de-schooling of society similar to that of Ivan Illich? Is it an example of what in German is called 'anti-Pädagogik', which amounts to a plea for the radical dismantling of the very idea of education and its institutions? We don't think so, and there are

a number of reasons for this. The first thing to bear in mind is ①
that Rancière's educational work is first and foremost a critique of
society, not of the school. Or, to be more precise, it is a critique of a
particular practice within society, namely the practice of explanation.
Where explanation happens does not really matter, the main point is
to highlight the anti-emancipatory effects of explanation wherever
explanation takes place with the intention to emancipate. In this
line of argument, 'the school' functions first and foremost as a
metaphor for the practice of explanation, and not as its necessary
or exclusive site.

Secondly, it is important not to forget that the argument that can ②
be found in Rancière's intervention is an argument about *emancipation*. To the extent to which Rancière's educational work can be read
as a critique of schools and schooling, it is therefore only a critique
of schools and schooling in so far as they aim to bring about emancipation by trying to overcome inequality. Some might argue that
schools have nothing to do in this domain anyway, so that in this
sense Rancière's critique is misplaced and misdirected. They might
argue that schools are simply there for the transmission of knowledge and skills, for the inculcation of values and for the production
of good behaviour. Rancière's critique suggests, however, that he
would reject such a narrow conception of the task of schooling.
Emancipation is still a crucial concern for Rancière – both for schools
and for society – but it is the particular logic of emancipation as the
overcoming of inequality that he rejects. In one sense, this places
Rancière's critique firmly within a tradition that does believe that
education has something to do and *should* have something to do with
emancipation, a tradition that, philosophically, runs from Kant to
Foucault and beyond, and that, educationally, runs from Rousseau
to such authors as Paulo Freire, Klaus Mollenhauer and Henry
Giroux. But whereas Rancière's shares an interest in emancipation
with authors like these, the logic of emancipation he proposes is a
radically different one.

Having said that there is a place for the school, and that such a
school should be emancipatory rather than explanatory, there is a
third point to bear in mind: Within such a school, there are schoolmasters – even potentially emancipatory schoolmasters. And there
are lessons, that is, lessons in intellectual emancipation. But what is no
longer there is the school as an institution for social emancipation, the
school as an institution for the eradication of inequality. The fact

that there is still a school and that there is still a schoolmaster in this school is actually quite significant. This is first of all because it signals that emancipation may still happen in schools – which is not to suggest that the school is the only place or the necessary place for emancipation. It is also significant because it reminds one that Rancière's critique does not operate on the all too easy opposition of teaching versus learning; an opposition in which teaching is seen as authoritarian, conservative and bad, and learning as liberating, progressive and good. Rancière's emancipatory schoolmaster represents a third option, so to speak, one which, in traditional educational language, is about the authority of the teacher, not about her absolute power over students. The difference is between the teacher who overwrites the speech of her students, who sees it as her task to explain to students what their speech actually means, and the teacher who reminds her students that they can already speak, the teacher who refuses her students the satisfaction of admitting that they are incapable of speaking.

Does all of this mean that schools which remain 'explanatory' should be abolished? Does this mean that there is no room for explanation in the school? The answer is both 'yes' and 'no'. Explanation, per se, is not wrong. Explanation does not automatically have a negative valence. It only becomes a problem in three cases. First, when it is construed as a vehicle for emancipation. Second, when explanation is taken for a metaphor as to how society is supposed to operate. Third, when explanation is assumed to explain how people actually learn things. Otherwise, explanation may happen. There is no problem in such happening. Explanation, like speaking within the realm of the distribution of the sensible – explanation can happen in all kinds of ways that are not hurtful to people, ways that are not hurtful to students in particular. Explanation – while not explaining how learning happens – may still be a *path* to learning. However, explanation is by no means a path to emancipation. It is here that we encounter one of the difficulties of schools and schooling in that the school is never just an institution for emancipation; it is also an institution for learning. Emancipation may therefore happen in schools, just as politics may happen in society, but emancipation is not something that can be produced or guaranteed. It is certainly not something to be explained. Emancipation is not the outcome of particular learning processes and trajectories – whether they be explanatory or otherwise – processes that claim to generate deeper insights into how things really are. There is, after all, not only nothing to *know* about inequality, there is also nothing to *learn* about it. In this sense, emancipation is entirely practical: It is about starting from a different assumption – the principle of the equality of all human beings, the assumption that there is no hierarchy of intellectual capacity – in order to see what can be done under such an assumption. This neither requires knowledge, nor learning, and certainly not explanation. Schools are thus optional.

WHAT IS THE WORLD IF NOT A SCHOOL?

Can a world that is not a school be imagined without dismay? It seems not. To see this, one need only notice that great march of explanatory progress called compulsory education. In developed parts of the world, for example, every child *must* attend school. Or if the child remains at home to be schooled, the child must nevertheless be schooled in some fashion. That the English term for taking one's child out of school – 'home-schooling' – retains its semantic ties to schooling is thus illustrative. One does not get away from schooling the child. The school rather changes venue and becomes the home. Since everyone begins as a child, it might well be said that 'the world is a school' wherever compulsory education exists. As long as every child must go to school, then the whole developed world has had the experience of school. And developed nations are not satisfied with the fact that all of *their* children are going to school. International development organizations work around the clock to make sure that more schools are opened wherever poverty is rife and children have no school to attend. Indeed, the march towards a humanity pedagogicized continues primarily because the explanatory regime is assumed to be beneficial for those it envelops. Because explanation appears as a positivity, as a good, anything short of explanation appears as a lack, as underdevelopement – and hence in need of remediation in the form of the school.

Perhaps the form of the school has been so ubiquitous for so long that it is difficult to imagine a world where the school does not operate. Perhaps this is why it is difficult for some people to think of *any* place, *any* thing, *any* idea or *any* person that does not need to go to school. Take the person of Jacques Rancière. Certainly, ill-receptions of Rancière's work, ones like the book review referred to earlier, signify that Rancière's disregard of school – that is to say his disregard for disciplinary boundaries – is difficult for some people to accept as a legitimate way to speak. Moreover, the efforts of academicians to pigeon-hole Rancière's work into particular discursive traditions – such as the discourse of political philosophy, or more particularly, the discourse of recognition – these efforts indicate an uneasiness with any unschooled version of Rancière's work. So, his work is either deemed wrong because it has not gone to school, or, it is deemed right, but just in need of schooling. Also, the many efforts to 'introduce' Rancière, whether they take the literal form of an introduction to one of his books, or the more general form of an introductory explanation of a thinker whose work is not yet widely known enough to *not* need introduction, these efforts too demonstrate another way to make sure that Rancière gets schooled. They demonstrate a general fear of a truancy. The book whose conclusion you are now reading might even be construed in a similar vein. It might be said that after all is said and done, a book such as this also performs a phobia of the unschooled. This book offers a window onto the thought of Rancière. Is it not an explanation? Is it not another school? We have tried to describe the way that this book is *not* a school. We have tried to describe this book as an intervention on, rather than a class on, Rancière's work. For some, the promise of such a distinction will not have been made good. For others, those who still want a schooled world, the distinction will not even be important or relevant. If the book has told a story, and if others can read the book and tell their own stories, then it will have been an intervention rather than a class.

But perhaps insistence on an explanatory order stems from a different place than the logic of development, or longstanding custom. Perhaps it comes from a fear that the word itself might be emancipated. As Rancière posits over and over, the word has no essential relation to truth. Truth is whole, and language fragments it. Truth is necessary and language is arbitrary. But as we have seen, the explanatory order will insist on a different relation between truth and the word. The school and all of its operators – whether they be traditional, progressive, or critical – assume that language represents and explains truth. And the school explains on a second order, namely, that the world constantly needs to be explained, and that it *can* always be explained. The school explains that the world is to be explained. In so doing, it explains that language can do such explaining. Thus if the world were not a school, it would be a place where language has no relation to truth. The world would be a place where the word is set free to circulate in ways that are not guided by the march of disciplines. It would be a place where people encounter words from proximity to proximity rather than from within the orderly queues of particular configurations of knowledge. It would be a place where childhood meanderings of thought are the order of the day, and where no measurements of evaluation could possibly apply. Any metric would be without metric, and all meanderings would be assumed to be equal. It is easy to understand then that the unschooled world is to be feared on another level. It is to be feared because it leads to what some might call epistemological relativism. An unschooled world where language is arbitrary is to be feared because such a world leaves each person in a place where there is no metric to adjudicate between one person's truth and that of another.

Finally, though, one must remember the following: The unschooled world is only feared by those who have been thoroughly schooled. The emancipated word has no enemies among the truant. None among children and none among artists. None among those who would take equality as a point of departure.

NOTES

CHAPTER 1

1. This essay, a translation by Charles Bingham, was originally presented at the Rio de Janeiro State University in June of 2002 at a conference entitled 'O valor do mestre – igualdade e alteridade na educação'. It is printed here with permission.
2. Unless otherwise indicated, quotations in this translator's introduction refer to excerpts from *On Ignorant Schoolmasters*.

CHAPTER 2

1. Describing his own method in the third person, Rancière writes: 'Let us sum it up: the works of Rancière are not "theories of," they are "interventions on." They are polemical interventions. This does not only mean that they take a political stance. This means that they imply a polemical view of what ideas are and do'. (Rancière 2009a, p. 116).
2. The Online Etymology Dictionary, http://www.etymonline.com (last accessed 11 March 2008)
3. The French word here is 'partage' which can either be translated as 'division' or as 'distribution'. Whereas 'distribution' highlights the fact that each particular distribution of the sensible gives everything a place, 'division' highlights the fact that subjectification redistributes the distribution of the sensible, and thus both distributes and interrupts.
4. In French, Rancière sometimes (but not always and not always consistently) makes a distinction that is difficult to translate (and that has not always been picked up by translators consistently) between 'la politique' and 'le politique'. The first refers to the domain of politics in the general sense, whereas the latter indicates the moment of the interruption of the police order ('la police' or 'l'ordre policier'). The latter, according to Rancière, is the 'proper' idea of politics and in several of his publications he has shown how particularly political philosophy but also particular forms of politics have tried to suppress the political 'moment'.
5. Although some of Rancière's writings may give the impression that he is primarily – or perhaps even exclusively – concerned about questions of inequality in relation to social class, Rancière's configuration of emancipation is definitely not restricted to this. Emancipation is about the verification of the equality of any speaking being with any other speaking being. Dissensus is therefore always about the redistribution

of the demarcations between 'noise' and 'voice', not in terms of a politics of recognition where those with a voice grant a voice to those who up till now were considered only to be able to produce 'noise', but on the basis of the 'simple' claim that one is producing 'voice' rather than 'noise'. We return to this in Chapters 3 and 7.

6. The idea of 'discussion partners' would assume that Rancière's work is just one voice with a space that is already defined. Rather than adding his voice to the discussion on emancipation, we might perhaps read Rancière's work, in his own words, as an intervention, or as a staging of dissensus. In this sense, we might see Rancière's work itself as a political act or act of politics.

CHAPTER 3

1. As Rancière puts it, 'Speaking animals are distant animals who try to communicate through the forest of signs' (Rancière 2002, this volume).

2. On the logic of the tort, or the logic of the "wrong," as it appears in English in *Disagreement*, Jean-Philippe Deranty has made this observation: 'As the etymology of the word *tort* tells us, Rancière's logic, the logic of the tort, is twisted logic. It is not dialectical logic leading to higher synthesis' (Deranty 2003, p. 142).

3. In a sense, it might be said that politics itself conceptualizes even as it refuses to be conceptualized. Politics stages an incursion onto the distribution of the sensible at the same time that it refuses to be staged *by* this distribution.

4. Rancière makes this point as follows in an interview published in *Rethinking Marxism*:

   Well, the point is that, precisely, you can't anticipate explosions. Or, if you anticipate an explosion, you precisely risk blocking or diverting it from its own law, from its own form of progression. It is true that education can provoke this form of explosion, but it's unclear whether you can predict the form of transformation and the way in which it becomes an explosion. (Rancière 2008, p. 411)

5. For additional commentary on Rancière's conception of equality in politics, pedagogy and aesthetics, one can look at Méchoulan, E. (2004) and May, T. (2008a, 2008b, 2007a).

6. Rancière describes his own breaking of disciplinary boundaries as 'indisciplinarity':

   My problem has always been to escape the division between disciplines, because what interests me is the question of the distribution of territories, which is always a way of deciding who is qualified to speak about what. The apportionment of disciplines refers to the more fundamental apportionment that separates those regarded as qualified to think from those regarded as unqualified; those who do the science and those who are regarded as its objects. (Rancière 2007b)

NOTES

7. Rancière identifies his linguistic project as one that is different both from the structuralist hermeneutics of suspicion and from a Derridean hermeneutics of infinite readings. Rancière's was inspired by the events of May '68. As he describes his linguistic project, 'My approach begins from a different reading of Plato's critique of writing [different from Derrida's]'. It is, rather:

> The availability of a series of words lacking a legitimate speaker and an equally legitimate interlocutor interrupts Plato's logic of 'the proper' – a logic that requires everyone to be in their proper place, partaking in their proper affairs. This excess of words' that I call *literarity* interrupts the relation between an order of discourse and its social function. (Rancière 2000, p. 115)

8. Recalling, for just a moment, Rancière's double use of the explanatory master and the oppressing master, it is worth noting that there, too, Rancière avoids the usual psychologizing account of the master-slave dialectic. Whereas usually the master-slave encounter is posed in terms of the alienation of the slave's consciousness, its subservience to the consciousness of the master, Rancière stands on its head this usual account by showing that the element of a shared linguistic understanding between master and slave is first and foremost a sign of equality rather than a tool of oppression. Thus, the linguistic equality of master and slave precedes any psychological account of alienation.

9. In an interview of 2009, Rancière compares his pedagogical ideas to a general notion of a pedagogy of the oppressed, not to Freire's work in particular. He points out the following:

> If there is a specific pedagogy of the oppressed, then it must be thought of as a specific case in the general idea of intellectual emancipation, because basically the idea of emancipation is the same for rich people and for poor people. (Rancière 2009b)

The generality of this statement shows it all the more worthwhile to insert Rancière's written work into a conversation with Paulo Freire's written work.

10. We would like to thank Hartley Banack on his thoughtful comments regarding the insidious side of educational psychology.

11. Rancière has addressed the foreclosure inherent in this tautology/must-be-helped dichotomy elsewhere, in his discussion of Hannah Arendt and the Rights of Man. As he notes,

> Either the rights of the citizen are the rights of man – but the rights of man are the rights of the unpoliticized person; they are the rights of those who have not rights, which amounts to nothing – or the rights of man are the rights of the citizen, the rights attached to the

fact of being a citizen of such and such a constitutional state. This means that they are the rights of those who have rights, which amounts to a tautology.

Either the rights of those who have no rights or the rights of those who have rights. Either a void or a tautology, and, in both cases, a deceptive trick. (Rancière 2004c, p. 302)

This situation is in fact identical to the situation of the oppressed student whose only chance at liberation stems from the very institution that is said to have oppressed him or her. Such a student, apparently, has no means outside of education (outside of the 'citizenry' of the school) to ascertain what freedom might mean to those who are already free.

12. Related to this movement of thought moving 'from proximity to proximity', Rancière has made the following comments about roaming through libraries and using the internet:

It is a question of having words circulate in free and desirable way, and I think this is what's happening with the internet. That is probably why some reactionary people are so angry with the internet, saying it's horrible that people log on to the web and they can find everything they want, that it is against research and intelligence. I would say no, it is the way intelligence, equal intelligence, works. You wander randomly in a library the same way you surf randomly on the internet. This is, from my point of view, what equality of intelligence means. (Rancière 2006b)

CHAPTER 5

1. As Honneth puts it, 'Fraser rightly uses the formula of "a dialectic of immanence and transcendence" – without, to be sure, in my view doing justice to what "transcendence" could mean' (Honneth 2003, p. 238).
2. This is Fraser's description of Honneth's position (Fraser and Honneth 2003, p. 45).
3. On ruling by lots, Rancière writes:

That is where politics begins. But that is also where, as it attempts to separate out the excellence specific to it from the sole right of birth, it encounters a strange object, a seventh title to occupy the superior and inferior positions, a title that is not a title, and that, the Athenian tells us, is nevertheless considered to be the most just: the title of that authority that has the 'favour of heaven and fortune': the choice of the god of chance, the drawing of lots. (Rancière 2006c, p. 40)

CHAPTER 6

1. While Rancière is here complimenting this Platonic style of the 'beautiful lie', he is also quick to note the irony in the fact that he is *not* condoning the content of Plato's beautiful lie. Writes Rancière,

   > at the moment when he most implacably states the organized distribution of conditions, he has recourse to what most radically denies it, the power of the story and that of the common language which abolishes the hierarchy of discourse and the hierarchies that this underwrites. (Rancière 2006a, pp. 10–11)

2. Elaborating on the poetics of politics – and thus on the necessity of the beautiful lie – and on his opposition to any particular political ontology, Rancière notes:

   > I think there's no general formula of Being from which the practices of art and politics can be deduced; that the prescriptive and the descriptive are always intertwined in such a way as to constitute the landscapes of the possible (those who describe reconfigure the possibilities of a world; those who prescribe presuppose a certain state of the world that is itself made up of sedimented prescriptions); and that the configuration of these landscapes is always, in the last instance a poem: an expression in ordinary language of the communal resources of thought. (Rancière 2007b)

3. It is helpful to note the limitations Rancière experiences when he tries to describe subjectification conceptually. These limitations are directly related to the difference between poetic narrative and predicative logic, a difference we are trying to highlight. In essence, Rancière is trying to describe a poetic event – subjectification – using the tools of predicative logic when he states, for example, that subjectification is a 'reconfiguration of the field of experience' (Rancière 1999, p. 35). This is a bit like saying, as if such a saying proves something, that the novels of Toni Morrison are a 'reconfiguration of the field of experience', and being satisfied with such a one line description.

CHAPTER 7

1. The word 'student', for example, seems to travel well in countries that have been affected by Latin. This may be less so for a word like 'learner', although there is, for example, the Dutch word 'leerling' which comes close in sound and meaning. A word like the French 'élève' is more difficult to translate into English. It stems from the verb 'élever', which means to lift up and, in this regard, exemplifies a logic that can also be found in some English words. We return to this below.
2. It is here that we can find a rationale for the French word 'élève'.

BIBLIOGRAPHY

Allan, J. (2003). *Inclusion, Participation and Democracy: What Is the Purpose?* Dordrecht: Kluwer.

Beetham, D. and Boyle, K. (1995). *Introducing Democracy. 80 Questions and Answers.* Cambridge: Polity Press.

Benhabib, S. (1996). Toward a deliberative model of democratic legitimacy. In S. Benhabib (ed.), *Democracy and Difference* (pp. 67–94). Princeton: Princeton University Press.

Biesta, G. J. J. (1998). 'Say you want a revolution . . .' Suggestions for the impossibile future of critical pedagogy. *Educational Theory 48* (4), 499–510.

—(2004). Against learning. Reclaiming a language for education in an age of learning. *Nordisk Pedagogik 24* (1), 70–82.

—(2005). What can critical pedagogy learn from postmodernism? Further reflections on the impossible future of critical pedagogy. In I. Gur Ze'ev (ed), *Critical Theory and Critical Pedagogy Today. Toward a New Critical Language in Education* (pp. 143–159). Haifa: University of Haifa.

—(2006). *Beyond Learning: Democratic Education for a Human Future.* Boulder, CO: Paradigm Publishers.

—(2007). Education and the democratic person: Towards a political understanding of democratic education. *Teachers College Record 109* (3), 740–769.

—(2009a). Good education in an age of measurement. *Educational Assessment, Evaluation and Accountability 21* (1), 33–46.

—(2010). How to exist politically and learn from it: Hannah Arendt and the problem of democratic education. *Teachers College Record 112* (2), 558–577

Bingham, C. (2002). Paulo Freire's debt to psychoanalysis: Authority on the side of freedom. *Studies in Philosophy and Education 21* (6), 447–464.

—(2008). *Authority is Relational.* New York: Suny Press.

—(2009) Under the name of method: On Jacques Rancière's presumptive tautology. *Journal of Philosophy of Education 43* (3), 405–420.

Bourdieu, P. and Passeron, J. C. (1979). *The Inheritors.* Chicago: University of Chicago Press.

Bourdieu, P., Passeron, J. C. and Nice, R. (1977). *Reproduction in Education, Society and Culture.* London: Sage Publications.

Brockliss, L. W. B. (1994). Review of *The Ignorant Schoolmaster. French Studies XLVIII*, 104–105.

Deranty, J-P. (2003). Jacques Rancière's contribution to the ethics of recognition. *Political Theory 31* (1), 136–156.

Dewey, J. (1910). *How We Think.* Boston: Heath. Republished 1991 by Prometheus Books, Amherst, NY.

—(1916/1944). *Democracy and Education. An Introduction to the Philosophy of Education.* New York: Free Press.

Dryzek, J. S. (2000). *Deliberative Democracy and Beyond. Liberals, Critics, Contestations.* Oxford: Oxford University Press.

Eagleton, T. (2007). *Ideology: An Introduction. New and Updated Edition.* London/New York: Verso.

Elster, J. (ed) (1998). *Deliberative Democracy.* Cambridge: Cambridge University Press.

Fraser, N. (1997). *Justice Interruptus: Critical Reflections on the 'Postsocialist' Condition.* New York: Routledge.

Fraser, N. and Honneth, A. (2003). *Redistribution or Recognition? A Political-philosophical Exchange.* London/New York: Verso.

Freire, P. (1970). *Pedagogy of the Oppressed.* New York: Continuum.

Fukuyama, F. (1992). *The End of History and the Last Man.* Harmondsworth: Penguin.

Gibson, A. (2005). The unfinished song: Intermittency and melancholy in Rancière. *Paragraph 28* (1), 61–76.

Gundara, J. S. (2000). *Interculturalism, Education and Inclusion.* London: Paul Chapman.

Gunn, J. S. (1965). *The Terminology of the Shearing Industry. Part 1 (A-L).* Sydney: University of Sydney, Australian Language Research Centre.

Gur Ze'ev, I. (ed)(2005). *Critical Theory and Critical Pedagogy Today. Toward a New Critical Language in Education.* Haifa: University of Haifa.

Gutmann, A. (1993). Democracy. In R. E. Goodin and Ph. Pettit (eds), *A Companion to Contemporary Political Philosophy* (pp. 411–421). Oxford: Blackwell.

Habermas, J. (1987). *The Theory of Communicative Action. Volume Two: Lifeword and System: A Critique of Functionalist Reason.* Boston: Beacon Press.

—(1988). *Theorie des kommunikativen Handelns. Erster Band.* Frankfurt am Main: Suhrkamp.

Hallward, P. (2005). Jacques Rancière and the subversion of mastery. *Paragraph 28* (1), 26–45.

Haugsbakk, G. and Nordkvelle, Y. (2007). The rhetoric of ICT and the new language of learning. A critical analysis of the use of ICT in the curricular field. *European Educational Research Journal, 6* (1), 1–12.

Held, D. (1987). *Models of Democracy.* Cambridge: Polity Press.

Hirsch, E.D. (1999). *The Schools We Need and Why We Don't Have Them.* New York: Anchor Books.

Honig, B. (1993). *Political Theory and the Displacement of Politics.* Ithaca, NY: Cornell University Press.

—(2001). *Democracy and the Foreigner.* Princeton, NJ: Princeton University Press.

Honneth, A. (1996). *The Struggle for Recognition: The Moral Grammar of Social Conflicts.* Cambridge, MA: MIT Press.

James, W. (2009). *Pragmatism.* Retrieved 2 August 2009. http://www. gutenberg.org/dirs/etext04/prgmt10.txt

Kant, I. (1982). Über Pädagogik [On Education]. In I. Kant, *Schriften zur Anthropologie, Geschichtsphilosophie, Politik und Pädagogik* (pp. 695–761). Frankfurt am Main: Insel Verlag.

—(1992[1784]). An answer to the question 'What is enlightenment?' In P. Waugh (ed), *Post-modernism: A Reader* (pp. 89–95). London: Edward Arnold.

May, T. (2007). Jacques Rancière and the ethics of equality. *SubStance 36* (2), 20–36.

—(2008a). *The Political Thought of Jacques Rancière: Creating Equality.* University Park, PA: The Pennsylvania State University Press.

—(2008b). Jacques Rancière: Literature and equality. *Philosophy Compass 3*(1), 83–92.

McLaren, P. (1997). *Revolutionary Multiculturalism: Pedagogies of Dissent for the New Millennium.* Boulder, CO: Westview Press.

Méchoulan, E. (2004). On the edges of Jacques Rancière. *SubStance 33* (1), 3–9.

Mollenhauer, K. (1976). *Erziehung und Emanzipation.* [Education and emancipation.] München: Juventa.

Mouffe, C. (1993). *The Return of the Political.* London/New York: Verso.

—(2000). *The Democratic Paradox.* London/New York: Verso.

The Online Etymology Dictionary, http://www.etymonline.com (last accessed 11 March 2008).

Pelletier, C. (2009). Emancipation, equality and education: Rancière's critique of Bourdieu and the question of performativity. *Discourse 30* (2), 137–159.

Rancière, J. (1991a). *The Ignorant Schoolmaster. Five Lessons in Intellectual Emancipation.* Stanford, CA: Stanford University Press.

—(1991b). *The Nights of Labour.* Philadelphia, PA: Temple University Press.

—(1995a). *On the Shores of Politics.* London/New York: Verso.

—(1995b). Politics, identification, and subjectivization. In J. Rajchman (ed.), *The Identity in Question* (pp. 63–70). New York/London: Routledge.

—(1999). *Disagreement: Politics and Philosophy*. Minneapolis, MN/London: University of Minnesota Press.

—(2000). Dissenting words: A conversation with Jacques Rancière. *Diacritics 30* (2), 113–126.

—(2001). Ten theses on politics. *Theory & Event 5* (3). Retrieved 5 March 2007. http://muse.jhu.edu.proxy.lib.sfu.ca/journals/theory_and_event/v005/5.3ranciere.html

—(2002). Sur "le maitre ignorant." Lecture given at the State University of Rio de Janeiro, 2002. Retrieved 5 December 2008. http://multitudes.samizdat.net/Sur-Le-maitre-ignorant

—(2003a). *The Philosopher and His Poor*. Durham & London: Duke University Press.

—(2003b). Comments and Responses. *Theory & Event 6* (4). Retrieved 28 August 2009. http://muse.jhu.edu.proxy.lib.sfu.ca/journals/theory_and_event/v006/6.4ranciere.html

—(2004a). *The Politics of Aesthetics*. London: Continuum.

—(2004b). Entretien avec Jacques Rancière. Entretien paru dans le No. 1 de la revue "Dissonance": "Beyond Empire." Mise en ligne le dimanche 18 Avril 2004. Retrieved 9 November 2008. http://multitudes.samizdat.net/article1416.html

—(2004c). Who is the subject of the rights of man? *South Atlantic Quarterly 103* (2/3), 297–310.

—(2006a). Thinking between disciplines: An aesthetics of knowledge. *Parrhesia 1*, 1–12.

Rancière, J. and Lie, T. (2006b). Our police order: What can be said, seen, and done. Interview published in *Eurozine* online. Originally published in English in *Le Monde diplomatique* (Oslo). Retrieved 22 August 2007. http://www.eurozine.com/articles/2006-08-11-lieranciere-en.html

—(2006c). *Hatred of Democracy*. London/New York: Verso.

—(2007a). The emancipated spectator. *ArtForum*, March 2007. Retrieved 5 January 2009. http://findarticles.com/p/articles/mi_m0268/is_7_45/ai_n24354915/pg_13/

—(2007b). Jacques Rancière and indisciplinarity. *Void Manufacturing*, posted on 15 October 2008. Retrieved 12 June 2009. http://voidmanufacturing.wordpress.com/2008/10/15/jacques-ranciere-interview-2007.

—(2008). You can't anticipate explosions: Jacques Rancière in conversation with Chto Delat. *Rethinking Marxism 20* (3), 402–412.

—(2009a). A few remarks on the method of Jacques Rancière. *Parallax 15* (3), 114–123.

—(2009b). Interview with Jacques Rancière. *Kafila: Media, Politics, Decent* (website). Retrieved 1 April 2009. http://kafila.org/2009/02/12/interview-with-jacques-ranciere/

Ravitch, D. (1995). *The Schools We Deserve*. New York: Basic Books.

Ruitenberg, C. W. (in press). Queer politics in schools: A Rancièrean reading. *Educational Philosophy and Theory*.

Tenort, H.-E. (2008[3]). *Geschichte der Erziehung. Einführung in die Grundzüge ihrer neuzeitlichen Entwicklung*. Munchen: Weinheim.

Torres, C. A. (1998). *Democracy, Education and Multiculturalism. Dilemmas of Citizenship in a Global World*. Lanham, MD: Rowman and Littlefield.

Warren, M. (1992). Democratic theory and self-transformation. *American Political Science Review 86*, 8–23.

Young, I. M. (2000). *Inclusion and Democracy*. Oxford: Oxford University Press.

INDEX